Effective Leadership Development

John Adair is an internationally recognised writer, teacher and adviser on leadership. His clients have included such organisations as ICI – the first British company to make £1 billion profit – Exxon Chemicals in the United States, Mitsubishi, Lehman Brothers, BAE Systems, British Airways, the Church of England, the Department of Education and many other organisations in both the private and public sectors. His 30 books, such as *Effective leadership* and *Not bosses but leaders*, have been translated into 18 different languages. For further information and contact details, see www.johnadair.co.uk.

The Chartered Institute of Personnel and Development is the leading publisher of books and reports for personnel and training professionals, students and all those concerned with the effective management and development of people at work. For details of all our titles, please contact the publishing department:

tel: 020 8612 6204

e-mail publish@cipd.co.uk

The catalogue of all CIPD titles can be viewed on the CIPD website:

www.cipd.co.uk/bookstore

Effective Leadership Development

John Adair

Chartered Institute of Personnel and Development

Published by the Chartered Institute of Personnel and Development,
151 The Broadway, London, SW19 1JQ

First published 2006

Typeset by Curran Publishing Services Ltd, Norwich, UK

Printed in Great Britain by The Cromwell Press, Trowbridge, Wiltshire

British Library Cataloguing in Publication Data
A catalogue of this publication is available from the British Library

ISBN 1-84398-133-5

Chartered Institute of Personnel and Development
151 The Broadway, London, SW19 1JQ
Tel: 020 8612 6200
E-mail: cipd@cipd.co.uk   Website: www.cipd.co.uk
Incorporated by Royal Charter. Registered Charity No. 1079797

■ CONTENTS

List of figures		ix
Part I	Leadership development in perspective	1
Introduction		3
Chapter 1	First thoughts	5
Chapter 2	The nature of leadership	9
	The qualities approach	9
	The situational approach	11
	The functional approach	12
	How far should leadership be shared?	17
	Conclusion	21
Chapter 3	Exploring leadership development	23
	The invitation	23
Part 2	The seven principles of leadership development	37
Introduction		39
Chapter 4	A strategy for leadership development	43
	What is strategy?	44
	The human factor	45
	The natural system of leadership development	46
	Overcoming the first hurdle, or over my dead body	47
	The second hurdle – you	48
	Leadership or management development?	49
	Key points	52

Chapter 5	**Selection**	**53**
	The right person for the right job	53
	Selecting team leaders	54
	Are there any psychological tests for leadership?	56
	Selecting operational business leaders	56
	Selection in perspective	57
	Key points	60
Chapter 6	**Training for leadership**	**61**
	The priority of team leadership training	62
	The hallmarks of high-volume, high-quality and low-cost team leadership training	63
	The auxiliary role of e-learning	65
	Outdoor leadership training for managers	67
	The other two levels of leadership	68
	Key points	71
Chapter 7	**A career development policy**	**73**
	On careers	74
	The hourglass model of career change	75
	The principles of succession planning	77
	Equal opportunities	79
	Key points	82
Chapter 8	**Line managers as leadership mentors**	**83**
	Can mentoring be developed?	84
	Developing the individual	85
	Key points	88
Chapter 9	**Self-development**	**89**
	Building a corporate culture that encourages leadership learning	89
	Teaching or learning?	90
	The strategic importance of books on leadership	91
	Key points	94
Chapter 10	**The strategic leader**	**95**
	The rise of the chief executive	96
	The chief executive's contribution to leadership development	97
	Your responsibility for the corporate culture	98
	A personal word to your chief executive	99
	Key points	101

Part 3	**Principles in action**	**103**
Introduction		**105**
Case study 1	Action-centred leadership in the Scottish Police *William Allan*	107
Case study 2	RAF use of action-centred leadership *Group Captain John Jupp*	111
Case study 3	Action-centred leadership in Armenia *Barry Chester*	115
Case study 4	Royal Navy leadership training and action-centred leadership: Leadership training of young officers at Britannia Royal Naval College (BRNC) *Commander Keith Harvey*	119
Case study 5	Action-centred leadership in the Army	131
Case study 6	Leadership development in higher education *Dr David Faraday*	137
Case study 7	Imperial Chemical Industries (ICI)	145
Parting thoughts		**151**
Appendix: List of basic leadership functions		**155**
Notes		**157**
References		**159**
Index		**161**

▪ FIGURES

2.1	The hierarchy of needs	15
2.2	Three overlapping circles of needs	15
6.1	The learning priority circle	66
7.1	The hourglass model of career change	76
9.1	The interaction between theory and practice	91
11.1	The three-circles model	113
11.2	The getting things done model	123
11.3	The continuing leadership challenge	126
11.4	The transferable functions of action-centred leadership	127

1 ■ LEADERSHIP DEVELOPMENT IN PERSPECTIVE

INTRODUCTION

"On every hand today the cry is for more and better leaders."

"What industry needs now is not bosses but leaders."

You may understandably think that both these remarks were made in the present. In fact the first comes from American author Ordway Tead's book *The art of leadership* published in 1935. As for the second, that was said to me by Vic Feather, the then General Secretary of the Trades Union Congress. The year was 1969, when Britain was already immersed in a decade of bitter and internecine conflict between management and organised labour.

Our *sense* of the need for leadership is much stronger in times of change, increased competition, conflict or uncertainty about the future. But the *need* itself is perennial, and I shall explain why that is the case later.

Today, not least because our awareness of change is so strong, many organisations are embarked upon the journey of trying to transform their managers into business leaders, while others are contemplating doing so and wondering what is the best way to go about it.

My solution to the problem as given in this book is twofold. First, you have to think very carefully about what leadership is. Second, you have to apply intelligently the seven principles of leadership development within the context of your own environment.

The business case for developing effective leaders is simple. Change isn't going to disappear – ever. To navigate the turbulent seas of change every organisation needs leaders at all levels – team, operational and strategic. The golden key to sustained success is to have great people working for you – and great leaders at all three levels.

Just reflect for a moment on your own experience of what a leader can do that someone lacking in leadership cannot. Think what a team can achieve with great leadership, compared with a work group labouring under pedestrian management. In office or factory, shop or call centre, human nature always responds and works best where there is good leadership. As John Collier said: 'Not geniuses, but average men and women require profound stimulation, incentive towards creative effort, and nurturing of great hopes.'

That theme – the need for great leaders at all levels – informs every page that follows. By the time you have finished reading this book you should have:

- a clear idea of the concept of leadership – the generic role of any leader and the essential attributes needed to fulfil it

- an idea of how individuals grow naturally as leaders as their career unfolds

- a sense of what organisations can do to work with this natural process and to develop the leaders they need for today and tomorrow

- the inspiration to create or progress a strategy for growing leaders.

You have a vitally important part to play in developing the leadership your organisation is now looking for. What this book will do for you is to equip you to lead the way in this particular field.

1 ▪ **FIRST THOUGHTS**

> "To be without leaders, to obey no one, is unworthy of man: it is to be like the animals."
>
> > Vietnamese saying, quoted in Frances Fitzgerald,
> > *Fire in the Lake* (1958)

What is leadership? Is it the same as command? How, if at all, does it differ from management? Clearly we need to be able to answer these questions before we can address the question of development.

There are, of course, literally thousands of books, articles and research studies – more than 150,000 of them since 1934 – which purport to answer those questions. If you and I had several lifetimes we should never complete a full 'literature review' on this subject. But take heart, as the eminent philosopher Gilbert Ryle wrote, 'Genius shows itself not so much in the discovery of new answers as in the discovery of new questions.' While we do not need to aspire to genius, the dictum is sound: rather than plough through 150,000 answers, our first step should be to identify the right question.

In fact I did find, or rather stumble upon, the right question, and everything else has stemmed from it. The question is a simple one:

> "Why is it that one person rather than another is accepted as leader in a working group?"

Fortuitously the question came to me just at the right time in history – roughly between 1945 and 1960 – when it was possible to identify three distinct ways of answering it. My contribution was to integrate these three approaches into a whole that was more than the sum of its parts, a chemical compound rather than a mixture. In this composite form I found the answer – well, 90 per cent of it – to the key question.

Now 90 per cent is sufficient – if the answer is correct – to design effective leadership *selection* and *training* programmes. So one important test of the answer was, *does it work to select or train leaders?* I am lucky: it did work and – 40 years later – it still does.

The first proving ground was the British Army. The first application of the composite 'answer' was to train for leadership: training young troop or platoon commanders-to-be. It took place at Sandhurst during the 1960s, under my general supervision as Adviser in Leadership Training. (I should perhaps explain that this was an unpaid appointment, over and above my 'day job' as a civilian lecturer in military history.)

Before I go on I probably need to answer the single biggest question that people have about my work. People often say to me something like, 'John, your ideas on leadership may work in the military but our organisation simply isn't like an army. We don't have the command and control culture, we don't have unquestioning obedience. If an officer tells his men to do something they do it – if I just "tell" my team to do something they probably won't. The world of work these days is much more consensual than the military. How can your ideas be relevant to my world?'

To this I have two answers. The first is that that the armed forces are a lot less authoritarian than most people outside the forces realise. It is actually very rare for a good officer to issue a direct order. Second, and more importantly, although the outward style and expression of leadership may change, depending upon the environment in which it operates, the underlying role, qualities and characteristics of leadership *are* generic. Several case studies later in the book will, I think, illustrate this. My ideas on leadership did not have to be developed in the army, it is just that in the 1960s that happened to be the most conducive place to work on leadership.

By 1964, after three years of trials, Sandhurst formally adopted the new approach, and not long afterwards the Royal Air Force and the Royal Navy followed suit. The working name for the short common training course based on it in the Services was *functional leadership*; later, when applied even further afield, it was called *action-centred leadership* (ACL).

The core of functional leadership is the generic role of leader, the role that is general and shared by all who may be defined as leaders – in any field or at any level or in any culture or at any time. My great discovery was that this universal could be refracted like light into three primary functions: achieving the task, building and maintaining the team, and motivating and developing the individual. For training purposes they could then be further broken down at team leadership level into six or seven functions, like the colours of the rainbow. Last, I was able to identify definitively some of the key personal qualities, as well as the distinctive knowledge and skills or competencies that fulfilling this generic role calls for in any leader.

Labels like 'functional leadership' and 'action-centred leadership' are useful as differentiators from the old exclusive reliance on the qualities approach (see Chapter 2). You should remember, however, that the compound theory – the whole which is more than the sum of the parts – that is a sufficient answer to the primary question actually has no name. That is not quite true, for it is *leadership*.

Another key idea to keep in mind is that in English the suffix '-ship' can mean either a role or an attribute. As a result the word 'leadership' can be used for both a role that a person (or a group of persons) occupies, and also as an attribute – such as when we say of someone, 'He showed real leadership.' This has caused a great deal of confusion about leadership among those who have studied it. What the integrated theory or philosophy that stems from my breakthrough in 1960–62 does for us, fortunately, is to unite these two senses of leadership.

Last but not least, the discovery of the generic role of leader simply bypasses like a beleaguered city the long and sterile continuing debate over the semantic differences between 'leadership' and 'management' which has preoccupied management academics, gurus and writers on the subject since it first erupted in the early 1970s. More on this later.

One problem I have is that I do not want to keep referring to my nameless composite answer to the basic question with long-winded phrases. Nor can I simply call it leadership, as I should like to do. The reason for that is linguistic: the word 'leadership' functions in the English language in several ways, and it would not serve the prime purpose of communication to use it as the label of an integrated theory, however sufficient or comprehensive that theory has proven to be.

Putting in another way, leadership like all personal relations, always has something unknown, something mysterious about it – 'the irrational tenth, like the kingfisher flashing across the pool', as T. E. Lawrence said. There is – and always will be – more to be discovered about it.

Most of us could not recite Einstein's special theory of relativity (which he originally outlined in just eight papers without footnotes), but we often do identify it by a symbol, the key equation $e = mc^2$ (which relates three factors or elements: energy, mass and the speed of light). In the social field, the general theory I developed is actually quite as complex as Einstein's, for it embraces no less than three sets of three: the three main approaches (qualities, situational, and group or functional) the three sets of need present in working groups, and three levels of leadership. Since this is not physical science, we cannot express all this as an equation. But the three-circles model (see p113) which relates to the complex interactions of task, team and individual, does serve as a symbol of the generic role of leader. It is the $e=mc^2$ of the leadership field, although perhaps a better analogy would be Crick and Watson's double helix. For it has the same simplicity and elegance, even beauty, as the latter, as well as that quality of truth which mathematicians call *deep*. For truth is always given, always there, but at the same time its depths can never be plumbed: there is always more to be explored. Truth is timeless but always timely. Anyone who has attained an element of truth has an enormous competitive advantage, not least as a teacher.

2 ▪ THE NATURE OF LEADERSHIP

Before we can discuss how to develop leadership we need to have an understanding of what leadership is.

▢ THE QUALITIES APPROACH

'Leaders are born, not made.' This is perhaps the most common assumption about leadership. Those who hold it maintain that there are certain inborn qualities, such as initiative, courage, intelligence and humour, which together predestine a person to be a leader. By the exercise of will-power, itself seen as an important leadership trait, or by the rough tutorship of experience, some of these qualities might be developed. But the essential pattern is given at birth.

Although there is a positive contribution to our understanding of leadership in this qualities approach, it suffers from several disadvantages as far as leadership development is concerned. The first is that there is no agreement upon what these 'qualities' may be. As long ago as 1940 one survey of 20 experimental studies revealed that only 5 per cent of the leadership qualities examined were common to four or more studies.[1] We have not got any closer to a consensus since!

The writers of one article (Allport and Odbert 1936) have listed 17,000 words used to describe qualities of personality. Although there has been a continual effort to boil down the qualities to those that are essential, lengthy lists are still common. At one military conference I was handed a list of 64 leadership traits. The world record must be held by the ill-starred Council for Excellence in Management and Leadership, which in 2001 produced a list of 83 attributes, condensed from a list of over 1,000. These long lists of 'competencies', as leadership qualities now tend to be known, are virtually useless for the purposes of development. When they are reduced to a smaller number – say less than 20 (as in the case of the NHS) – they become more general. But if they are not grounded in the generic role of *leader*, they lack intellectual coherence and seem arbitrary, so they have little credibility or practical value. My estimate is that organisations in both the public and private sectors in Britain have wasted some £20 million on commissioning management consultants to produce these near-worthless lists.

Besides this lack of consensus over the qualities of leadership, there is a second major disadvantage to this theory. The qualities approach, whether in its old traits form or its new 'transformational' competencies clothes, is ill suited to act as a basis for leadership training. Intrinsically it hardly favours the idea of training at all, and instead encourages a concentration on selection. The ability to recognise a born leader becomes all important, and attempts to 'make' leaders are viewed with suspicion.

In fact, how could the 'qualities of leadership' be used in training? The teacher or trainer might speak in the language of traits to the student, but it is difficult for the latter to know what to do with such remarks. If told, for example, that one lacks a sense of humour, how does one develop it? By watching successful comedians at work? No, there is nothing more serious than someone bent on improving his or her sense of humour, and nothing more self-centred than this cultivation of one's own personality. And in the long run self-centredness is the one certain disqualification for any form of leadership. At the worst an unskilful teacher, using the 'qualities of leadership' language, can do incalculable harm. A comment such as 'Jane, you lack decisiveness' is hardly likely to improve Jane's ability to make decisions.

One usually finds that students who have attempted self-development based on the traits approach have abandoned it after a few weeks, either in despair because they have not attained the desired qualities or (much worse) in pride because they believe they have. The pattern is often that followed by a young manager known to the author, who resolved to practise numbers 1 to 5 on the issued list of 32 'leadership competencies' on Mondays, numbers 6 to 10 on Tuesdays, numbers 11 to 15 on Wednesdays, and so on. By Friday he had completely forgotten Monday's quota, and had become so dispirited that he abandoned the Herculean task.

Therefore the qualities assumption does not form a good basis for leadership training programmes, but it does have other uses. First, it reminds us that natural potential for leadership varies in individuals. Second, many of us need the language of qualities to transfer our knowledge of a person's leadership ability to someone else. Third, this approach emphasises the importance of what the leader is as a person, in an age that may be inclined temperamentally to skate over the importance of character as opposed to personality. Today we do know more about the qualities that are essential in a leader, such as enthusiasm and integrity, but there is still no reason to make the qualities (or competencies) approach the main basis for a training course.

THE SITUATIONAL APPROACH

Besides revealing the inadequacies of the traits analysis of leadership, the social scientists investigating the subject in the late 1940s began to underline the importance of the *situation* in determining who would become a leader in a given group. R. M. Stogdill (1948), for example, who studied the evidence for 29 qualities appearing in 124 studies, concluded that although intelligence, scholarliness, dependability, social participation, and socio-economic status were found to bear some relation to leadership:

> "the evidence suggests that leadership is a relationship that exists between persons in a social situation, and that persons who are leaders in one situation may not necessarily be leaders in other situations."

This finding expressed what might be called a *situational approach* to leadership, namely which person becomes, or should become, the leader of a group depends on the particular task, the organisational and the environmental setting. Another study by W. O. Jenkins, published a year earlier in 1947, supports this conclusion. After reviewing 74 studies on military leadership the author wrote:

> "Leadership is specific to the particular situation under investigation. Who becomes the leader of a particular group engaging in a particular activity and what the leadership characteristics are in the given case are a function of the specific situation. There are wide variations in the characteristics of individuals who become leaders in similar situations and even great divergence in leadership behaviour in different situations. The only common factor appeared to be that leaders in a particular field need and tend to possess superior general or technical competence or knowledge in that area. General intelligence does not seem to be the answer."

To illustrate this theory let us imagine some shipwreck survivors on a tropical island. The soldier in the party might take command if natives attacked them, the builder lead during the work of erecting houses, and the farmer might direct the labour of growing food. In other words, leadership would pass from member to member according to the situation. 'Situation' in this context means primarily the task of the group.

There are two drawbacks to this approach as far as training leaders is concerned. First, it is unsatisfactory in most organisations for leadership to change hands in this manner. At one time the Royal Air Force veered towards this doctrine by entertaining the idea that if a bomber crashed in a jungle, the officer who took command for the survival operation might be not the captain of the aircraft, but the person most qualified for the job. But role flexibility to this degree, in most work organisations, tends to create more problems than it solves.

Second, an explanation is needed for the fact that certain men and women seem to possess a general leadership competence which enables them to exercise an influence over their fellows in a whole range of situations. Of course, the compilers of trait lists had been seeking, without much success, to analyse this general aptitude, and there was no denying its reality. Even so, by seeing leadership not as a quality but as a relationship, and by grasping the importance of the leader possessing the appropriate technical or professional knowledge required in the given situation, the proponents of this approach made a most valuable contribution to our understanding of the subject.

As a result of my own researches, we now know that Socrates was the first to articulate this situational approach, in ancient Athens. He pointed out that where women knew more than men – he instanced the weaving industry in Athens – they were accepted as leaders. This observation was no doubt more astonishing 2,400 years ago (or even 30 years ago) than it is today, when women are leading Royal Navy warships, FTSE 100 companies and government departments.

THE FUNCTIONAL APPROACH

So far the research work described has been largely literary: the analysis and comparison of books and articles on leadership. In the late 1930s, however, more objective research commenced into the behaviour of actual small groups, both in what were described as 'laboratory' conditions and 'in the field', in an attempt to bring the scientific methods of observation, hypothesis and verification by experiment to bear upon the phenomena of social life.

These studies have produced a vast crop of papers on the social psychology of small groups, including the leadership displayed in them. From this wealth I selected an interesting theory, which might be called 'the theory of group needs', as having the greatest potential relevance to leadership training. By combining and developing this theory with the positive contributions of the two earlier and complementary approaches – qualities and situational – I managed to achieve a comprehensive and integrated understanding of the role of leadership. To grasp the concept of generic leadership, it is necessary first to look at the even more basic or foundation concept of *group needs*.

If we look closely at any working group, we may become aware of its distinctive corporate life, its difference from others even in the same organisation. By analogy with individual human beings this could be called the 'group personality'. But according to the theory of group needs, just as individuals differ in many ways and yet share certain common attributes and needs, so also do the corporate entities or social organisms which we know as groups. Let us now examine the most important of these group needs.

Task

With reference to working groups, the most obvious group need is to achieve the common task. Generally speaking, all such groups come together consciously or unconsciously because the individuals in them cannot alone achieve an objective. For example, one person, by his or her own efforts could not reach the moon; therefore a team is assembled for the job and co-operation becomes essential.

But does the group as a whole experience the need to complete the task within the natural time limits for it? Just as people are not very aware of their need for food if they are well fed, a group will be relatively oblivious of any sense of need if its task is being performed successfully. In this case the only sign of a need having been met is the satisfaction or elation which overtake the group in its moments of triumph, a happiness which as social beings we may count among our deepest joys, especially when we look back on an arduous journey, successfully completed.

Before such a fulfilment, however, many groups pass through a 'black night of despair' when it may appear that the group will be compelled to disperse without achieving what it set out to do. If the members are not committed to the common goal this will be a comparatively painless event; but if they are, the group will exhibit various degrees of anxiety and frustration. Scapegoats for the corporate failure may be chosen and punished; reorganisations might take place and new leaders emerge. Thus adversity reveals the nature of group life more clearly than prosperity. In it we may see signs or symptoms of the need to get on effectively with whatever the group has come together to do.

Team

Second, in order to achieve the common objective the group must work as a team. Therefore it needs to be maintained as a cohesive unity. This is not so easy to perceive as the task need; like an iceberg, much of the life of any group lies below the surface. The distinction that the task need concerns things and the second need involves people does not help overmuch. Again, it is best to think of groups that are threatened from without, by forces aimed at their disintegration, or within, by disruptive people or ideas. We can then see how they give priority to maintaining themselves against these external or internal pressures, sometimes showing great ingenuity in the process. Many of the written or unwritten rules of the group are designed to promote this unity and to maintain cohesiveness at all costs. Those who rock the boat, or infringe group standards and corporate balance, may expect reactions varying from friendly indulgence to downright anger. Instinctively a common feeling exists that 'united we stand, divided we fall', that good relationships, desirable in themselves, are also essential means towards the shared end. This need to create and promote group cohesiveness we may call the *team-maintenance* need.

Individual

The third area of need present in the corporate life inheres in the individual members rather than in the group itself. To the latter they bring a variety of needs – physical, social and vocational – which may or may not be met by participating in the activity of the group. Probably physical needs first drew people together in working groups: the primitive hunter could take away from the slain elephant a hunk of meat and a piece of hide for his own family. Nowadays the means for satisfying these basic needs of food, shelter and protection is money rather than kind, but the principle remains the same.

There are however other needs, less tangible or conscious even to their possessors, which the social interaction of working together in groups may or may not fulfil. These tend to merge into each other, and they cannot be isolated with any precision, but Figure 2.1 indicates their character. Drawn from the work of A. H. Maslow (1954),[2] it also makes the point that needs are organised on a priority basis. As basic needs become relatively satisfied the higher needs come to the fore and become motivating influences.[3]

These needs spring from the depths of our common life as human beings. They may attract us to, or repel us from, any given group. Underlying them all is the fact that people need each other, not just to survive but to achieve and develop personality. This growth occurs in a whole range of social activity – friendship, marriage, neighbourhood – but inevitably work groups are extremely important because so many people spend so much of their waking time in them.

Figure 2.1 The hierarchy of needs

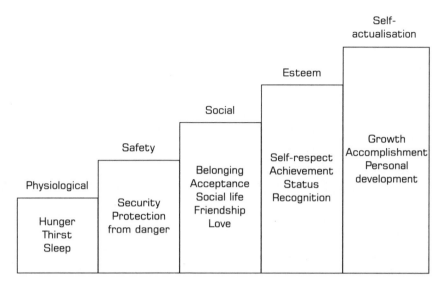

The interaction of needs

These three areas of need cannot be studied in watertight compartments: each exerts an influence for good or ill upon the others. Thus we may visualise the needs as three overlapping circles as in Figure 2.2.

Figure 2.2 Three overlapping circles of needs

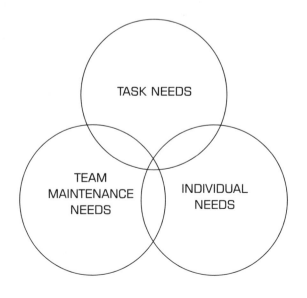

If you place a disc over the 'task' circle it will immediately cover segments of the other two circles as well. In other words, lack of task or failure to achieve it will affect both team maintenance, for example by increasing disruptive tendencies, and also the area of individual needs, lowering member satisfaction within the group. Move the disc on to the 'team maintenance' circle, and again the impact of a near-complete lack of relationships in the group on both task and individual needs may be seen at a glance.

Conversely, when a group achieves its task the degree of group cohesiveness and enjoyment of membership should go up. Morale, both corporate and individual, will be higher. And if the members of a group happen to get on extremely well together and find that they can work closely as a team, this will increase their work performance and also meet some important needs which individuals bring with them into the common life.

These three interlocking circles therefore illustrate the general point that each area of need exerts an influence upon the other two; they do not form watertight compartments.

Functions

Clearly, in order that the group should fulfil its task and be held together as a working team, certain functions will have to be performed. By 'function' in this context we mean any behaviour, words or actions which meet one or more spheres of the group needs, or *areas of leadership responsibility* as they may also be called. Defining the aim, planning, and encouraging the group, are examples of what is meant by the word 'function'.

In most small groups the responsibility for the performance of such functions rests with the designated leader, though this is not to say that he or she is expected to perform them all him or herself. Nor can we assert that there are certain functions which must always be supplied, for this depends upon the situation in the widest sense, including the task and the nature of the group.

By contrast with the traditional view that a leader must 'possess' certain traits or qualities which make him or her stand out in any company, the functional approach stresses that leadership is essentially an interaction between leader, group members and the situation. Yet the personality of the leader is not ignored in this functional approach. It may often serve the group by representing the qualities valued for both corporate survival and the completion of the task. Thus military officers ought to possess courage, the cardinal military virtue, and team leaders in NHS hospitals should exemplify the four or five qualities expected in all nurses, but in both cases this will not in itself make them leaders. Perhaps Sir Winston Churchill in the Second World War afforded the classic example of the 'representative function of character', as it could be called. His bulldog demeanour and resolute speech personified the spirit of a nation, just as surely as did the youthful vigour of President Kennedy represent the mighty energies of the United States 20 years later. Still, the functional approach lays emphasis not upon what the leader is in terms of traits, or upon what he or she knows of the appropriate technical knowledge, but upon leaders' ability to provide the necessary functions in a manner acceptable to the group: that is, what they actually *do* to lead in response to the three overlapping areas of task, team maintenance and individual needs.

HOW FAR SHOULD LEADERSHIP BE SHARED?

The question of how far designated leaders should share their leadership functions with group members deserves consideration. Not many leaders consciously think this problem out; most accept the assumptions on the matter prevalent in their organisation, although in some cases these are ripe for review. Supposing, however, that leaders became aware that there were alternative patterns from which they could choose, what would be the factors they should consider before deciding on one or other of them?

In a classic answer to this question two writers, Tannenbaum and Schmidt, in the *Harvard Business Review* (1958) suggested three: the leader himself or herself, their subordinates and the situation. Let us look at each of these in turn:

The leader

The personality of the designated leader – interests, aptitudes and temperament – will exert an influence on the pattern of shared leadership in any group. Also, what leaders believe about human nature and life – their values – determines much. If the leader regards people as things to be used for one's own ends, pawns on the chessboard, then he or she will not see much need for consultation. If the leader is temperamentally lazy, or just plain incompetent, he or she might well allow group members a greater share in leadership functions than either their experience or the requirements of the situation dictate.

Perhaps the critical factor in the temperament of leaders is the degree to which they feel secure in an uncertain situation. 'The manager who releases control over the decision-making process thereby reduces the predictability of the outcome,' the *HBR* authors write (Tannenbaum and Schmidt 1958):

> **"**Some managers have a greater need than others for predictability and stability in their environment. This 'tolerance of ambiguity' is being viewed increasingly by psychologists as a key variable in a person's manner of dealing with problems.**"**

'Know thyself,' enjoins the Greek philosopher. By looking at their own experience, the reactions of others, and the comments of friends, leaders should gain a modicum of self-knowledge. They should be aware of any bias in their character; for example, whether or not they tend to be too task-centred and correspondingly less conscious of the needs of individuals, or whether they operate most efficiently and effectively in one pattern of shared functions rather than another. The end of such study is more appropriate action. Like an archer 'aiming off' into the wind, leaders can then make allowances for these unseen tendencies in their character when they perceive that a particular situation demands a different kind of response from their normal one. Although they may feel it 'unnatural' to share out or arrogate to themselves leadership functions (as the case may be), this will not be the judgement of others if they have appreciated the situation correctly.

The subordinates

The obvious question here for leaders to ask themselves is how far the group members possess the necessary knowledge, experience and skill relevant to the problem in hand to participate satisfactorily in leadership functions. At one end of the scale a class of very junior schoolchildren clearly lack the qualifications to decide how they are going to plan out their work; it has to be done for them by the adult leader. On the other hand, a team of highly skilled technicians will not require this degree of spoonfeeding on how to tackle a common task; the steps may become evident to all of them at once. Leaders therefore should take into account the degree of expert knowledge, experience and social skill resident in the group as the second main factor in their appreciation.

One note of caution, however, should be sounded at this point. Some leaders rationalise their temperamental preference for a pattern by claiming 'their' group is incapable of being more than submissive or dependent followers. In those cases the leaders concerned lack sufficient self-knowledge to discern their own guiding motives. In fact it is rarely true that a group is so devoid in all respects of any leadership potential that one man or woman must do it all for them; this is sometimes a fiction created as a piece of self-justification by a domineering personality.

Moreover, entrusting the inexperienced with a share in leadership functions is often the only way of giving them the necessary experience, and of motivating them to acquire the appropriate knowledge and skill. There is nothing more mysterious and exciting than this ability of good leaders to transform their followers: without it, a vital element, the light and life of leadership, is missing. The great leader is always aware of latent powers in people which can be evoked and harnessed: he or she responds to these like a water diviner, thereby meeting an important segment of individual needs.

As a general principle, the more members participate in decisions, the more they feel motivated to carry them out; and the more they share in the life of the group. In this way, the more chance there is that their potentialities as persons will be fulfilled. Therefore, one element of empowerment is sharing decisions with the team and each individual as far as it is realistically feasible to do so.

The situation

There are, however, limits to which leaders can go in this educative process without a denial of their own responsibility, and these are set by the situation. 'Situation' in this context must again be understood in a wide sense, embracing group task and the working environment. When we think of an important (predominantly) task function such as decision-making, it is clear that in certain situations life or death may depend on the speed of a group's reaction. In such cases it is appropriate for leaders to retain or concentrate decision-making in their own hands rather than share it with the group. In fact some research shows that in hastily formed groups responding to crisis situations, for example serious motor accidents and forest fires, not only is decisive leadership tolerated from one person, but it is also positively expected. On the other hand, even in a crisis great leaders seem to find time to listen to their own team as well as others. It is worth remembering that a person can tell you a lot in one minute.

Consequently, we shall not be surprised to find that groups that habitually or character-istically operate in crisis situations exhibit a certain pattern of leadership, with the designated leader in a clear position of authority, and team members trained and disciplined to obey his or her orders promptly and without discussion. Obvious examples of such groups are operating theatre teams, emergency services units, the crews of aircraft and ships.

But the stress element is not solely related to life and death; sometimes decisions must be taken promptly in order to avoid great loss to an industrial company. Time pressures may not always allow managers to share decision-making with their team as much as they may like to. That will be accepted as long as it is not the manager's own poor habits of time management that have led to the crisis!

Although the characteristic situation influences the general pattern, it does not arbitrarily fix it on a given point. Fire-fighter unit commanders, for example, in the station and on training exercises will act towards their team in such a way as not to betray the residual authority they need to command when responding to an emergency, but they would be unwise to behave in those situations as if a fierce fire were raging and the building was about to collapse. There is a flexibility within any pattern, which the good leader will exploit according to the *specific* situation, without detriment to his or her prime responsibility in the *characteristic* one. Indeed, a chair of a committee may range widely with an appropriate pattern during the confines of a two-hour meeting, or even within the context of five minutes.

Any given decision, then, can be compared to a cake that can be shared in variously shaped slices: between the leader and either the team as whole or an individual member. There is no fixed point (or 'style') in which every decision should be shared: it all depends upon factors in the situation, the group and the leader. The right or appropriate way is the one that does justice to all the relevant factors; and getting it right every time calls for good judgement in both the leader and the team.

Around the 1950s it was common – especially in Britain – to assume that decision-making and leadership were the same thing. That is why the so-called 'styles of leadership' – 'authoritarian', 'democratic' and 'laissez-faire' – which derived from one small and suspect American psychological study of decision-making in a youth club context in the 1940s – came to be applied confusingly to leadership in general. But we could equally construct a continuum to illustrate the amount of member involvement in, say, team maintenance functions. Indeed, very often leaders who exercise virtually all the task functions themselves will delegate (or be expected to share) many team-maintenance functions to other members of the group. In an infantry platoon, for example, the platoon sergeant rather than the platoon commander often responds to the other two areas of need, holding the men together as a group and making sure that as individuals they get food and mail where possible. In less formal groups – a factory production team, for example – those sharing in leadership in this way may not be designated, but nevertheless they will act to complement the functions performed by the appointed leader.

As a general principle, in any group larger than five members, some degree of sharing becomes essential. There is so much functional activity required for the group to work effectively on the task without losing cohesion and without individual needs being overlooked that the appointed or elected leaders simply cannot do it all themselves, and they must therefore share with or delegate to others.

Now we have rejected the nonsense that there is one politically correct point or style, which a leader must observe when making all decisions, is there still a place for the concept of style in leadership? Of course. Just as the style of your handwriting is unique to you, so is the particular or distinctive way in which any given leader fulfils his or her generic role of leader in a field. In other words, while the three circles and constituent functions remain constant, every leader is different and unique in his or her manner of performance. Each has his or her own style, and very different styles within the broad frame of a democratic ethos can be equally effective. The generic role of leader is like a black and white X-ray: it needs the colour of your personality to give it life and particular form – to make it a creative art. In that sense, as Lord Sim once said, 'Leadership is just you.'

CONCLUSION

You can see that we have come a long way since 1952, when an American psychologist C. A. Gibb (1954) concluded his review of over 30 years of research in the United States into the subject of leadership by stating that:

> "any comprehensive theory of leadership must incorporate and integrate all of the major variables which are now known to be involved, namely (1) the personality of the leader, (2) the followers with their attitudes, needs and problems, (3) the group itself ... (4) the situations as determined by physical setting, nature of task etc.... No really satisfactory theoretical formulation is yet available."

In this chapter the simple concept of 'functional leadership' has been outlined not so much to meet the academic need mentioned by Gibb, but to serve as a basis for more effective leadership training.

Thanks to the breakthrough in Britain in 1960, symbolised by the three-circles model, we know have a 'satisfactory theoretical formulation', one that has withstood the tests of experiment and experience for over 40 years. Nothing can be certain, but it now looks like the three circles and the associated generic role of leader is actually true. And truth is the rock-like foundation we need if we are to design lasting and effective strategies for leadership development.

> "A leader is a person with the qualities (personality and character) and the knowledge appropriate to his or her field, who is able to provide the

necessary functions for a group or organisation to achieve its task, work as a team and for the needs of the individuals to be met – not in isolation but in sharing functions with the team. The leader is accountable, but all are animated by the same sense of responsibility for the three circles.**"**

That self-evidently is not a neat definition, but it is a way of drawing the threads of this chapter together.

3 ▪ EXPLORING LEADERSHIP DEVELOPMENT

▯ THE INVITATION

Recently I was asked to speak to a small branch of the CIPD in the north of England. Their interest, they said, was in leadership development. 'Your model has now been available for 40 years,' they wrote, 'and there are a number of questions we want to put to you. We hope that you don't mind being put on the spot.'

I assured them that I had no objection to that. In order to make it a discussion – I have given up lectures with slides or PowerPoint long ago – we agreed to limit the numbers of participants to about 12. They all undertook to read one or other of my key books on the subject which are available, and I also sent them copies of *Training for leadership* (Adair 1968), *Action-centred leadership* (Adair 1973a) and *Developing leaders* (Adair 1988).

We met for dinner at a splendid inn appropriately named the Nelson Arms (Nelson once remarked how odd it was that people were calling inns the Nelson Arms, seeing he had only one arm). Over dinner I briefly outlined for them the generic role of leadership, and all that I had built on that foundation. Then they asked me the following questions.

Have you thought of modifying or changing the three-circles model?

There has been no need. Some people add a wider circle around it labelled 'context', others alter it in acceptable ways in the process of making it their own. My job is to be a steward, to hand it on to the next generation, who may make better use of it than we have been able to do so far.

In fact when people start altering their models they often do so for the worse.

Tannenbaum and Schmidt, for example, produced a revised and more 'politically correct' version of their 1959 article – one of the key satellite theories in the three-circles constellation – in the *Harvard Business Review* in 1973. Judge for yourself, but I think it inferior stuff. First thoughts are often best, even if foxed with a few of the yellowish-brown stains of time.

One danger of releasing the three-circles model in *Training for leadership* (1968), like three coloured balloons on the winds of time, is that people even manage to get a simple model like this one wrong. I just assumed, of course, that everyone would naturally place the 'task' circle on top, as I always do. Not so. It is common to see the model upside-down. (Just look on the Internet under 'action-centred leadership'.) Moreover, the circles should always be drawn the same size, with a proper overlap. That doesn't mean that they should always have an equal share of the leader's attention – that depends on the situation. You have to be flexible, but the model is like a compass – it will bring you back on course.

Still on the three-circles model, which is the core of your practical philosophy as well as its symbol: how do you know it is true?

The truthful answer is that I don't. What I do know, however, which I did not know in 1968, is that the three-circles model has lasted; it has withstood the test of time. Forty years is quite a long time. Can you think of any model or theory in our field of which that can be said? It is worth pursuing your question in the context that philosopher's call epistemology – the study of the nature and grounds of knowledge, especially with reference to its limits and validity.

The dominant paradigm nowadays tends to be the epistemology of science. The tradition in science is that one advances a hypothesis which, gaining credence, turns like a caterpillar to butterfly into a theory. The theory is then subjected to further controlled experiments and, if it defies all efforts to disprove it, the implicit claim to be accepted as knowledge is substantiated.

'The separation of the true from the false by experiment or experience,' said the Nobel-laureate physicist Richard P. Feynman, 'that principle and the resultant body of knowledge which is consistent with that principle, that is science' (Gleick 1992, p126). Notice that the truth status of that body of knowledge is far from absolute. The philosopher Sir Karl Popper (1976) expressed this clearly:

> "The empirical basis of objective science has thus nothing 'absolute'
> about it. Science does not rest upon a solid bedrock. The bold structure

of its theories rises, as it were, above a swamp. It is like a building erected on piles. The piles are driven down from above into the swamp, but not down to any natural or 'given' base; and if we stop driving the piles deeper, it is not because we have reached firm ground. We simply stop when we are satisfied that the piles are firm enough to carry the structure, at least for the time being."

So much for the epistemology of science. But how about other domains of human intellectual endeavour – my own, for example? How can we possibly know that the three-circles understanding of leadership is *true*?

Feynman gives us an important clue in his phrase 'experiment or experience'. Einstein (who once attended a lecture delivered by the young Feynman) develops it further:

> "Ethical axioms are found and tested not very differently from the axioms of science. *Truth is what stands the test of experience.*"

Einstein's principle, which I have here placed in italics, is further simplified in an old English proverb: *Time tries truth*. In this context, experience implies a knowledge based on considerable actual practice. Experience comes from the Latin verb *experire*, to try. An *experienced* person is one made skilful or wise through observation of, or participation in, a particular activity or affairs generally.

To meet the test of time the three-circles general theory has had to jump at least five big fences:

■ **Coherence of definition.** Does the concept or theory in view include what is commonly known about leadership and exclude what is commonly understood as not being leadership? Yes, it does.

■ **Consistency.** As in natural science, any new theory or model must not contradict what is already known or firmly established. Is there evidence that the theorists in question have built on what is already known, rather than trying to reinvent the wheel? Does their theory give a better and more comprehensive understanding, incorporating what are now seen to be the inadequate theories of the past? Yes, all these tests have been met.

■ **Sustained use.** Has it manifestly withstood the test of time? After, say, 10 years, has its reputation spread on the grapevine or has it faded? Who has used it successfully for more than 10 years? Has it survived criticism? The reputation of the three-circles model has grown, and so far it has survived its critics.

- **Teachability.** Is it clear, simple and comprehensive? Can it be taught to non-academics in such a way that the end-user is more effective as a leader? There is ample evidence that my work meets that requirement.

- **Transferability.** In this context by 'transferable' I mean that teaching the theory does not require the presence of its originator – or highly-trained colleagues. The aircraft has to be capable of being flown by ordinary pilots, not just the designer or the test pilot. Have others, apart from the inventor, conducted successful programmes or courses? What is lost in that transfer? Again, this test has been met.

You can see why it is only now – some 40 years after the generic leadership role was discovered and formulated – that we can now begin to celebrate. To have discovered truth, the quest of all thinkers, is thrilling. Moreover, truth hardly needs to be sold or marketed. It is self-propagating. As Sophocles said, 'Truth is always the best argument.'

What is the difference between a leader and a manager?

Given the great intellectual breakthrough I have been describing, this question is a category error, like asking what the difference is between fruit and strawberries. In *Training for Leadership* (1968), I wrote:

> "Essentially leadership lies in the provision of the functions necessary for a group to achieve its task and be held together as a working team. Now this is basic, the raw 'silver' called leadership, which to some extent may be separated and analysed in functional terms. But in reality leadership always appears in a particular form or 'vessel' which can be distinguished from others. This shape is fashioned above all by the *characteristic working situation* of the group or its parent organisation. To some extent the degree of participation in decision-making by group members may be used as a measure to contrast these different forms of leadership, but there are other variables as well. In the military *milieu* the shape which leadership assumes is best called 'Command'; in the industrial and commercial situation it is known as 'Management'. Two boughs from the same trunk, they can easily – but should not be – confused.
>
> In particular the modern industrial situation dictates a necessary technical knowledge for the leader. Besides the particular knowledge required for the firm or branch of business or industry in which he finds himself, the manager should also possess a general technical knowledge of the way in which scientific techniques can be systematically employed

for the efficient use of resources. But management techniques do not qualify a man for leadership in industry. They are only effective as extensions of leadership functions. Far from occupying a remote corner in 'industrial sociology' or 'industrial relations', leadership is *the* integrating concept, relating and binding together those subjects which are loosely grouped together as 'Management Studies' in business schools and universities.**"**

Forty years later – osmosis takes a long time – that insight has become the popular truism of today. The collapse of managerialism has been as spectacular and as unexpected as the collapse of communism. As Russia was, incidentally, run on managerialist lines there is a link between these two phenomena of our times.

You remember that I distinguish – or rather the English language distinguishes – between leadership (role) and leadership (personal attribute). *Role* is a metaphor from the theatre. From the French *rôle*, literally a roll, it was a part played by an actor or singer. Thence it came to mean function in the broadest sense. In fact in the case of leadership that role (or function) can be further refracted into a set of related functions. (See Appendix.)

In both its theatrical and more general social sense *role* can be understood in terms of *expectations*. It is what others expect from us, both vocationally and generally, that determines role. For example, you have some clear expectations of what doctors or police officers might say or do (and might not say or do) in their roles. If there is more than one person with expectations, roles can become quite complex, even giving rise to the phenomenon of *role conflict.*

In the most simple and atomic form of group – a free-standing group, like a street gang – the only expectations of the person who is leader come from the group members. In an organisational context the expectations are those of subordinates, superordinates (or superiors) and co-ordinates (or peers). It follows that the more all these parties agree on the role, the less likely it is that role conflict will arise.

Of course people in any of those categories can entertain unrealistic expectations of the leader role and/or of the person occupying it. Quite a lot of so-called leadership theory – 'transformational leadership' for example – falls into that category. Those unwieldy and overpowering lists of 'leadership competencies' that were fashionable two or three years ago simply fed the unrealistic expectation that only a Superman or Superwoman could become a leader.

The generic role of *leader* is at the core of being a manager or commander, or indeed any other headship office in an organisation. Whether or not the role-holder has leadership (personal attributes) is a secondary question. Who is to judge?

The office-holder may, for example, be convinced that he or she is a leader in that second sense. He or she may be right. But without going to the lengths of a formal 360-degree appraisal, here is a simple test: do people ever use the word 'leader' about this person? For in everyday use as an attribute – an attribute is what one infers as a characteristic of a person –' leader' carries some distinctive overtones:

> **"**A *leader* is one who is voluntarily followed because of an ability to guide and control others or because he/she has been chosen by a group or party to be its head. One tends to think of a leader as having arrived at his or her position chiefly because of his or her talent for influencing others and for acting as a guiding force.**"**

Contrast 'leader' with 'master'. In its commonest sense a master is a person who has been given the authority to enforce obedience, but the word does not suggest the innate ability of the leader to guide and influence others. 'Leadership' is our name for that innate ability that a leader has. The suffix '-ship' here indicates not so much status, official position or rank, or the collective members of a group, but *skill or expertise in a certain capacity*.

Hence this key principle: *you can be appointed a manager or commander, but you are not a leader until your appointment is ratified in the hearts, minds and spirits of those who work with you.*

You said that a role is comprised of expectations. Surely people never expected managers to be leaders – they were not paid to be, were they?

No, they were not. The origins of management as we know it lay in the nineteenth century, when there was the increasing employment of a body of paid agents – recruited mainly from the professions of accountancy and engineering – to administer increasingly large business concerns. In England these became known as the *managers* or the *management*, as distinct from public agents who were called (from residual reference to the monarchy) *civil servants* or, more generally, the *bureaucracy*. The highest level of the bureaucracy up until quite recently was known as the *administrative* grade, with managers as a subordinate rank below the administrators.

The role of these administrators – their know-how was variously called industrial, hospital, personnel and business administration (hence the MBA – Master of Business

Administration) – was modelled on the military command structure. Some big companies like Shell even called their higher-grade luncheon places 'messes' like the military.

The discovery of the generic role of leader in terms of the three-circles model actually created a sea change in people's expectations. Gradually, as osmosis worked, it became accepted, for example, that teambuilding and teamleading were expected of a (good) manager. Before 1968 the word 'team' was not in the dictionary of management. And in the course of time these expectations actually transformed the role of manager towards the leadership equation as I formulated it in the late 1960s. It is a case of a theory informally and indirectly bringing about a change in the very idea of what it means to be a manager.

Before 1968 the prevailing presumption was that 'management' was a civilian form of command. 'Managers' were surrogates for the master (owner) or the boss – in his (and it *was* male) absence they stepped into his shoes. Various evangelistic efforts were made in both America and Britain – to *add* leadership to the role of manager. But no one perceived that you didn't have to add it, for it was there already beneath the surface. It was a sleeping princess, awaiting the kiss of life.

How was the kiss of life administered?

Very simply. The first step in leadership training is to tell people what the generic role of *leader* is. By tell, of course, I don't mean lecture them: more help them to discover it. As Peter Drucker once put it to me, the first question a person should ask himself is, what am I being paid for? Functional leadership and action-centred leadership did just that, but in a way that was vitamin-enriched by a whole practical philosophy of leadership.

As Socrates taught us so long ago, people are on the whole well-intentioned. The reason that they are not effective as leaders is not lack of desire or willingness to be a good leader, it is ignorance. They do not *know* what the role requires. And they do not know because they have been left to guess; no one has taught them in the sense of helping them to think it out clearly for themselves. Much of our knowledge of leadership is common sense, and it merely needs to be put in better order so that people can make more use of it. But the three-circles model, the principal catalyst for transforming the complexities of leadership into something that is simple without being simplistic or superficial, is not the product of common sense. That had to be given to us.

Once the basic role is clear, there is a foundation to be built upon. Or, to change the metaphor, the acorn can then grow into an oak. For the principles of leadership are the same at all levels of leadership responsibility: what changes is complexity and intellectual requirement.

You mention levels of leadership. Can you say how this idea arose?

Of course. In fact in 1968 I envisioned that leadership development would one day happen at all levels of management. In *Training for leadership* I wrote:

> "it is important to make a general point, namely that leadership training can take place on various levels corresponding to the basic tiers of management. From the standpoint of training this book on the whole is concerned with the first level, the introduction of the student to the subject. Courses on this level may perhaps be best given to those who are about to take up their first main appointment which requires them to act in the role of leader. There is wide agreements that the lecture as a principal means of instruction is of limited value at this level, compared with the use of small group practical work with comment.
>
> In the 'middle management' area one would expect more emphasis upon the functions of leadership, such as *delegating* and *co-ordinating*, which become especially important when one is dealing with subordinates who are themselves leaders of groups. In addition on such courses much attention could be paid to the theory and practice of both analytical and creative thinking, for the leader's intellectual ability in these two spheres becomes steadily more important as his responsibilities grow. Although some progress has been made in the study of thinking and the ways of developing clear and creative thought there can be little doubt that much more research is both required and possible.
>
> At this level also, it is necessary that leaders should also understand much more about their responsibility for locating, releasing and developing the leadership potential of those under them. Besides practical group exercises, case-studies and observation of films on these themes and others, a course at this stage – lasting perhaps a week – could fruitfully include a higher content of lectures on relevant topics.
>
> The senior level of management, however, may also profit from an advanced study of leadership at the summit of large organisations. Moreover, men and women in this category need to know the concepts of leadership guiding their junior and middle managers, both in order to know what is going on and also so that they can employ a common

language in which to pass on their experience and wisdom to their subordinates.

In summary: The corporate leadership in any large organisation goes by different names but the heart of it is always a response to the task, the team maintenance and the individual needs of the organisation. In the services this corporate leadership goes by the name of 'Command'; in industry it is called 'Management'. The scientific techniques used by management are servants to the primary functions of leadership.**"**

In 1968 those words were visionary. No one thought like that. In his black-and-white, no-nonsense, call-a-spade-a-spade way, Field Marshal Viscount Montgomery told me as much. Forget it, he said, you haven't a chance. In a handwritten letter to me shortly after the book appeared, he wrote:

"Leadership is an immense subject. Nowhere is it more important to teach it than at Sandhurst and in universities; in fact to the young, *since it falls on dead ground with the older generation.***"**

Incidentally, Montgomery – whom many regarded as a born leader – certainly believed that leadership could be learnt. He wrote a book about it, *The path of leadership* (1961), and gave a lecture to the University of St. Andrews on 'Military Leadership'.

Well, can leaders be trained?

Some will say that leaders are born, not made, and that you can't make a leader by teaching, or training. I don't agree with this entirely. While it is true that some men have within themselves the instincts and qualities of leadership in a much greater degree than others, and some men will never have the character to make leaders, I believe that leadership can be developed by training. In the military sphere, I reckon that soldiers will be more likely to follow a leader in whose military knowledge they have confidence, rather than a man with much greater personality but with not the same obvious knowledge of his job. To the junior leader himself the mere fact of responsibility brings courage; the mere fact that by his position as the recognised head of a group of men he is responsible for their lives and comfort, gives him less time to think of his own fears and so brings him a greater degree of resolution than if he were not the leader. I know I found this to be the case myself in 1914, when as a young lieutenant I commanded a platoon and had to lead them in charges against entrenched Germans, or undertake patrol activities in no-man's-land. By the training I had received from my superiors in peacetime, I gained confidence in my ability to deal with any situation likely to confront a young officer of my rank in war; this increased my morale and my powers of leading my platoon, and later my company.

In other words, it is almost true to say that leaders are 'made' – rather than born. Many men who are not natural leaders may have some small spark of the qualities which are needed; this spark must be looked for, and then developed and brought on by training. But except in the armed forces this training is not given. In civilian circles it seems to be considered that leadership descends on men like dew from heaven; it does not. There are principles of leadership just as there are principles of war and these have to be studied.

Field Marshal Viscount Montgomery (1961)

In the 1960s and 1970s one spoke of junior, middle and senior management. Below junior managers were industry's NCOs, the warrant officers (supervisors) and the corporals (foremen). Against a backcloth of 'us' versus 'them' – unions against management – it was a political battle to persuade the industrial NCOs that they were part of 'us' and not 'them'. Industry, banks and public service organisations were inflated with managers and manpower: there were many grades and ranks of managers in the hierarchies of these bureaucracies. Managerial redundancy, unknown in the 1960s, was a social stigma you kept quiet about when it began to happen to a few individuals in the late 1970s. You can see that the climate was not favourable for leadership. It was only in the 1980s, as layers of corporate fat were shed, that I could see clearly the bony structure of the three levels of leadership – team, operational and strategic – beginning to appear. Already in *Effective leadership* (Adair 1983) I could write:

> "Leadership happens on different levels. Originally work on leadership focused upon the small group. Recently my own work has extended the functional leadership concept to leaders at all levels within the sphere of work, including the chairmen and chief executives of organisations employing more than 100,000 people.
>
> According to the well-known 'Peter Principle', people tend to be promoted to the level of their incompetence. Some people are perfectly

good leaders at one level, but they are less able to cope at the next level up. What can help you to determine your own level is your ability to appreciate the subtle changes which take place in the task, the team and the individual as you go higher up the mountain.

The three circles still apply. In the task area the top leader is concerned more with longer-term and broader aims. In the team area he has the double job of building and maintaining his immediate team of senior executives, and promoting a sense of unity among the diverse parts of the organisation. These two jobs are clearly inter-related. Again, the individual for him is both a senior leader – a known person in the senior team – and also each individual in the organisation. The latter will not be known personally or even by name in organisations of more than 500 people, but the top leader still needs to think constantly about that individual – and talk to him whenever possible."

It was an Indian professor of management at a conference in Penang who told me that the three-circles model would not become a general theory until it was applied not just to small working *groups* but to *organisations*. Although I began that process in *Effective leadership* (Adair 1983), it was not significantly advanced until the publication of *Effective strategic leadership* in 2001, where I identified for the first time the generic role and seven functions of a strategic leader. That opened the door to the possibility of training – well, at that level, education.

Your thesis is really that the key to successful leadership development is to give people training in the generic role of leader – the package of ideas symbolised by your three-circles. Did it work? How was it evaluated?

Trainers were much keener on evaluation in the 1970s than they are today. If you look at *Training for leadership* (Adair 1968) and *Action-centred leadership* (Adair 1973a) you will see how much attention was given to checking out not just immediate post-course reactions – which was done systematically, recorded and analysed – but also evidence of sustained use and value up to two years after the functional leadership or ACL course.

Neil Wates, chairman and chief executive of Wates the construction company, was the first person to ask me to try out the generic leadership role theory: I conducted three courses for site foremen on a building site next to Wates's head office in Croydon. These experiments, together with another series for female managers in Dorothy Perkins, were recorded and evaluated in *Training for leadership*. Principally through the agency of my work at (and later with) The Industrial Society, over one million managers experienced the ACL course in the 1970s and 1980s, not only in the United Kingdom but throughout the world.

If you glance at it now you can see that I sounded in 1973 as if I had completed my own task, and to be truthful that is how I felt at the time. Functional leadership was firmly rooted in the armed services – it is still the basis of leadership training today – and I had trained The Industrial Society to be both the principal missionary and also the main provider – with a trainer's manual as an aid – of both ACL courses and 'train the trainers' programmes.

Professionally in the 1970s I supported myself with experimental work in training managers in, first, decision-making, problem-solving and creative thinking, and second, communication – subjects of two of my early books, *Training for decisions* (Adair 1969) and *Training for communication* (Adair 1973b). For, together with leadership, I saw these two topics comprising the 'big three' of what Douglas McGregor had called 'the human side of enterprise'. To these I had added the first book in Britain on the desirability of teaching business ethics and how to do it – *Management and morality: some problems and opportunities of social capitalism* (Adair 1974). As an author I then turned back to writing history books.

All this changed when the adjutant-general of the British Army (the former commandant at Sandhurst while functional leadership was being introduced), said casually to me one evening over dinner, 'We ought to create a university chair for you in leadership.' That sounded to me a good idea, but Sir John Mogg could only promise moral support – no money. The chief of the Defence Staff, Marshal of the Royal Air Force Sir Neil Cameron – a former Spitfire ace who as assistant commandant at RAF Cranwell had been the prime mover in Cranwell's adoption of Functional leadership, arranged and chaired my 1967 lecture to the Royal United Services Institute and organised Britain's first ever conference on leadership training – confirmed as much.

Business – United Biscuits, Shell, the Dulverton Trust and the Prudential – provided the £40,000 then needed to fund a five-year professorial appointment, and I chose the new University of Surrey out of the only two universities who showed any interest. Thus I became the world's first professor of leadership studies – the latter phrase I coined for the occasion. A year later, incidentally, Harvard Business School, having accepted a multi-million dollar gift from Japan, announced that it had established the Konosuke Matsushita chair in leadership, its first holder being the psychotherapist–management thinker Abraham Zaleznik, who was already on the staff.

"We are going to win and the industrial West is going to lose: there is nothing much you can do about it, because the reasons for your failure are within yourselves.

Your firms are built on the Taylor model; even worse, so are your heads. With your bosses doing the thinking while the workers wield the screwdrivers, you're convinced deep down that this is the right way to run a business."

Konosuke Matsushita, Tokyo 1979

That appointment heralded the beginning of the leadership revolution in America. Having totally rejected the concept of leadership as vested in an individual person during the 1960s and 1970s as being anti-democratic and therefore un-American, the Americans suddenly did a 180-degree turn and created what has become known as the leadership revolution. Why? Because the impact of Japanese competition – with better leaders and better-quality management – woke them up. Thus it was the Americans who got the leadership bandwagon rolling in the 1980s, bedecked in the Stars and Stripes. Through the 1990s and into the present century the leadership-not-management movement gained even greater momentum.

The British followed a different path, a trail that I had blazed in the 1960s and 1970s. By the 1980s, having discovered the generic role of a leader 20 years before, we were ready to move on to the next stage of the journey: to move from the concept of *training* leaders on the three-circles principle to the much wider and more complex one of *developing* or growing leaders.

2 THE SEVEN PRINCIPLES OF LEADERSHIP DEVELOPMENT

▪ INTRODUCTION

"It takes a whole village to raise a child."
African proverb

Any organisation that seeks to develop leaders should give thought – strategic thought – to what I call 'the essential framework for any effective leadership training programme'. The first organisation that endeavoured to do that outside the military field was Imperial Chemical Industries (ICI) in the 1980s, but many others have followed. The ICI story, along with other case studies from a variety of organisations, can be found in Part 3 of this book.

From my experience with ICI, and subsequently, with many other non-military organisations in all fields and in all parts of the world, I have distilled this framework into seven principles:

1. A strategy for leadership development.

2. Selection.

3. Training for leadership.

4. A career development policy.

5. Line managers as leadership mentors.

6. Self-development.

7. The strategic leader.

Visualise the seven principles as being like the laws of aerodynamics. There are many different sizes and types of aircraft, but if they are to fly all have to obey the laws of aerodynamics.

▌ EXERCISE

Before you read about the seven principles complete the checklist on page 41. After you have read and re-read them, come back to the checklist and see if you wish to modify them. In the light of your answers, identify the *top five priorities* for your organisation on the next page – the *action plan*, followed by the *personal steps* you can take in that direction.

CHECKLIST

DOES YOUR ORGANISATION DEVELOP LEADERS?

	YES	NO
Do you have a clear strategy for building good human relations that includes developing leadership at every level?	☐	☐
When selecting people for management jobs do you assess them in terms of their functional ability (task, team and individual) and the associated qualities of personality and character?	☐	☐

Are appointed leaders given a minimum of two days of leadership training?

Always ☐   Sometimes ☐   Never ☐

	YES	NO
Do you have some system for career development, so that future senior leaders broaden their experience and knowledge?	☐	☐
Are all line managers convinced that they are the real leadership trainers, however effective they are in that role?	☐	☐
Is there a specialist 'research and development' team who are keeping the organisation and its line managers up to date and up to the mark?	☐	☐
Has your organisational structure been evolved with good leadership in mind?	☐	☐
Do leaders, actual or potential, realise that they are the ones who 'own' the problem of self-development?	☐	☐

In the light of this book so far, would you say that there was room for improving the organisational ethos?

A great deal ☐   Some ☐   None ☐

Are your top person and key team really behind leadership development?

Whole-hearted ☐   Half-hearted ☐   Not yet ☐

◼ ACTION PLAN

Organisation:...

Date:..

The top five priorities in order of importance are:

1

2

3

4

5

My personal steps to make it happen are:

(i)

(ii)

(iii)

"It is better to begin in the evening than not at all."

English proverb

4 ■ A STRATEGY FOR LEADERSHIP DEVELOPMENT

"A business is the reflection of the people within it."
Roger Falk

The seven principles are not equally applicable by everyone. Obviously, all of us can apply Principle 6, but Principles 1 and 7 are really the preserve of the strategic leader, the chief executive (officer) or CEO. (The Latin *officium*, meaning service or duty, comes from *opus*, work and *facere*, to make or do. It is a position of authority to exercise a public function and to receive whatever emoluments may belong to it.)

Fairly central to being a CEO in any field is one's accountability for strategy. Again it is helpful to be clear about terms. 'Accountability' is a legal or quasi-legal concept: if things go wrong, whose head is on the block? Who resigns or gets the sack? 'Responsibility' overlaps with it but is broader, and can be interpreted as being more subjective. It may be even clearer if we talked about having a *sense of responsibility*.

Obviously the strategic thinking, direction and planning of a nation, institution or organisation is too important to be left totally to one person, however exalted in office. The danger of having a great misleader is too great. That is why we have parliaments, senates, cabinets, boards of directors and strategic leadership team meetings, not to mention elections. Everyone working in an organisation has a stake in its strategy, but the leading role in the drama of formulating strategy undoubtedly belongs to the strategic leader. That is partly why he or she is paid a lot more money in salary, share options or privileges and the like than anyone else in the organisation. At national level it is the role of president or prime minister.

It is worth remembering that the phrase 'strategic leader' is relatively new; I coined it in the late 1970s. Before then 'strategy' was rarely used outside the military context; the traditional word in public administration and business was 'policy'. In fact policy and strategy are not quite synonyms. A policy is a general decision that guides one in making other decisions, as in 'our policy over immigration'. Strategy implies an end which is pursued by means.

Moreover, on the military model, (strategic) planning was the preserve of a large staff in the centralised head office bureaucracy, rather like the general staff – the 'brain of the army' – at headquarters.

WHAT IS STRATEGY?

The Greek word for a general was *strategos*. Strategy comes from a Greek word which means the art of being a commander-in-chief. The Greeks held that such generalship – as we might translate it – was essentially a higher form of military leadership. In fact 'strategy' combines two Greek words: *stratos*, a large and spread-out body of people such as an army, and *-egy* which means leader. The first syllable of our English word 'hegemony' has it too.

Even those, of course, with no knowledge of military history use the distinction between *strategy* and *tactics*. Tactics are limited and short term, covering such matters as methods of employing forces in battle. The word implies actions or means for accomplishing ends of less magnitude or at a shorter distance from a base of operations than those of strategy. By contrast, strategy implies a bigger canvas: the larger purpose together with much more comprehensive thinking and planning over a longer time scale for achieving it. Strategy is not actually more important than tactics, they are just means and ends on different scales.

A lesson in strategy

Field-Marshal Viscount Montgomery leaned forwards across the lunch table. 'What is the first rule of strategy?' he demanded of me. 'You won't find it in any book. I learnt it by hard experience.'

Needless to say, Monty did not need much encouragement to supply his own answer! It went as follows:

> **"**The commander-in-chief must be sure that what is strategically desirable is technically possible with the resources at his disposal.**"**

A decade later I recalled these words. A chief executive of a major company sat across the lunch table. He told me about a disastrous attempt at diversification. 'I learnt by hard experience,' he said, 'that it's no good taking over a company if you don't have management expertise in that field. We were way out of our depth.'

People, especially managers, are the key resource of a business enterprise. What is strategically desirable cannot be achieved unless the people available have the necessary knowledge, training and skill to make it happen.

The almost military sense of strategy came to be seen as more and more relevant to the world of business. Business is 'a war without an enemy' – competitors get even stronger and better organised; markets grow ever more demanding. Only the fittest survive. At the same time there are tighter 'rules of engagement', legal and moral penalties against those, like Robert Maxwell or Enron, who abandon integrity in search of short-term profits.

THE HUMAN FACTOR

You don't have to be a genius to see that the human factor – people – is a vital ingredient in strategic success, whatever your equivalent is to victory. It is not the only factor, note, but it is a most important one. The reason is that people are the sources of all energy and power, including brainpower. Machines produce power, but who makes, services, minds and replaces the machines?

If you cast your eye back over 2,500 years of military history the lesson is blindingly obvious. The winning combination is what the French call *matériel* – technology, equipment, wealth – and *personnel*, a body of persons employed in an organisation. Especially where no competitive advantage is enjoyed with regard to *matériel*, then having an edge in personnel becomes absolutely crucial.

In an army the *personnel* can be distinguished roughly as *leaders* and *soldiers*. The latter – their fitness, discipline, training and morale – are obviously critical, but so much of that and their performance in battle depends on their leaders. As Euripides put it succinctly:

> **"**Ten soldiers wisely led,
> Will beat a hundred without a head.**"**

The work of military leaders is not, of course, restricted to leading their soldiers from in front into battle, important as that primary act is. They are the ones who select, train, discipline and organise the soldiers in preparation for war. Incidentally, it is also true to say that good soldiers train their leaders. I know many officers who, as young subalterns, were taught how to lead by their platoon sergeants.

You can now see why getting the leaders right is so strategically important in an effective army. Not only do officers, commissioned and non-commissioned, create the right body of soldiers, but they also play an often key role in the development of *matériel* in all its forms.

Thus there is a great deal of truth in the military proverb, *there are no bad soldiers, only bad officers*. When Nelson's friend Collingwood was told that unrest on his ship was beginning to amount to mutiny, he exclaimed: 'What? A mutiny on my ship! Then it is my fault and the fault of every one of my officers.'

THE NATURAL SYSTEM OF LEADERSHIP DEVELOPMENT

A critical constituent of the *personnel* of any organisation, then, is its leadership – the corps of those men and women who occupy the *leader* roles at team, operational and strategic levels.

Who owns the problem of selecting and training team, operational and strategic leaders? Obviously it is part of the function of strategic leaders to select and train operational leaders, who in turn will choose and develop those chosen to be team leaders. Fine. But who ensures that an army has good strategic leaders?

The answer, of course, is that in a way no one does. What happens – or should happen – is that the best of the operational leaders, those with the intellectual and personal capacity, become strategic leaders. They have the brains, will and experience to do it.

Now on the way up these stars will have learnt the hard way that those who occupy the roles of leader ought to be leaders that their subordinates will respect and follow. They certainly would not have got to the top without being such leaders themselves. Therefore they naturally use their superior officer power to weed out bad leaders, appoint good ones and to do all within their capability to train or develop tomorrow's leaders. That is how it should be.

You will notice that there is an implicit 'chicken-and-egg problem' here. Team/operational leaders are the seedbed of strategic leaders; strategic leaders are the ones who shape team/operational leadership.

Until a decade or two ago non-military organisations did not know about, consider relevant or employ the natural system of leadership development. They did, of course, have a hierarchy of managers. Managers got promoted. Promotions were by seniority, the principle of 'Buggins' turn' or promotion by length of service rather than on individual merit. In technical fields promotion to manager went to those with technical or professional knowledge. The factor of leadership hardly ever came into the equation. Leadership, as I commented above, was seen as a military quality, not relevant to the world of business or the public service.

That picture has changed unexpectedly and dramatically in the last two decades. There is no shortage of awareness of the need for more and better leaders. But how do you transform managers into what they should be, *business leaders*?

It certainly helps if you have a strategy for leadership development at boardroom level. But there are two potential obstacles in the way: the chief executive is one, and the other is – you. You, that is, if you happen to be a director or a senior manager of human resources.

OVERCOMING THE FIRST HURDLE, OR OVER MY DEAD BODY

You may be inclined to throw in the towel here when we are only half-way through Round One of a ten-round boxing match. 'But John, if you could meet our chief executive .... Well, he/she is. ...'

'Useless?' I suggest.

'No, not at all – well-respected, competent, doing a good job, but not "into" leadership or stuff like that. I agree with what you are saying but I could never persuade our executive board to even find time to discuss leadership development, let alone debate and agree upon a strategy.'

You have to be realistic. The older generation who are in the boardroom now – men and women in their 40s and 50s – were formed before the need for real leadership became so apparent. They underwent no training for leadership at team level. They came in on the coat tails of a generation that believed blindly that as they had got to the top they were by definition leaders. Leaders like themselves, they say, were born, not made. Others might need leadership development, but not them: the fact that they are at the top is evidence that they are leaders. Is it?

But things are changing fast. A senior manager told me that his chief executive, the son-in-law of the owner of a family business employing 5,000 people, had at first rejected the strategy for leadership development he had submitted to the board. A few days later he was summoned for coffee and the CEO told him, 'It's too late for me, you can't teach an old dog new tricks, but I see where you are coming from. Go ahead, develop a strategy for leadership development. I am not particularly for it but – if you think that is the right thing to do – I shall not block you at the strategic planning budget committee stage. Keep me informed.'

You can actually achieve a great deal over the dead body of your chief executive, providing he or she doesn't deposit it in your pathway.

▉ THE SECOND HURDLE – YOU

I am assuming now, for a moment, that, as I said above, you are director of human resources or head of personnel or some such equivalent in your organisation – the chief staff officer (people). If the chief executive and your fellow executive directors give you a general strategic directive to put your organisation into the front rank of those that really do develop leaders, could you do it?

If your answer is 'no' or 'don't know', pray tell me what you are being paid to do. Industrial relations? Yes, but that is only no more than 10 per cent of your time. Recruiting and training the 'troops'? All the paperwork and administration attendant upon employment and compliance with legislation? Surely you have a department or administrative/training staff to whom you can delegate all but certain policy issues in those camps. Your key role is to *think*, to think about *personnel* in relation to the *strategic* and progressive conduct of the business. Is there a strategy for leadership development? Who manages it on behalf of the organisation and under the overall direction of the chief executive? If that isn't your responsibility, whose is it?

Case study: the National Health Service

Almost 1.3 million people – or the equivalent of the combined populations of Birmingham and Coventry – now work for the NHS, which is the world's biggest

---

employer after Indian State Railways and the Chinese Army (although it is worth noting that both of those workforces represent a far smaller proportion of their national populations than NHS employees do of the United Kingdom's). 59,000 new staff joined the NHS last year.

There are 386,400 nurses – matching the entire population of Edinburgh – 109,000 doctors and 122,100 scientists and other therapists. Half of all employees are fully qualified clinical staff, while 16 per cent provide support to keep hospitals and other NHS organisations running, such as cleaning, catering and IT. There are 38,500 managers.

The NHS is organised into about 350 trusts, each with a chief executive, and there are 28 strategic regional authorities, headed up by chief executives who report to the NHS chief executive in the Department of Health.

Exercise in strategic thinking

Imagine that the chief executive of the NHS has asked you to sketch out a strategy for developing more effective leadership at all levels and all parts of the business – clinicians and nurses as well as managers. What would you tell him that the NHS needs to do? Identify five priorities that seem self-evident. You may like to revisit this page and revise your answer after studying Principles 2 through 7.

LEADERSHIP OR MANAGEMENT DEVELOPMENT?

Just to be clear, a strategy for leadership development is not an added extra to management development. A line manager is in the generic role of *leader*. Leadership development in the narrower sense begins when both that generic role and the attributes required to perform it are opened up, the comprehensive set of leadership functions is taught, and an opportunity for practising them with increasing skill is provided. On that foundation, to be acquired logically at team leader level, other layers of understanding develop like a crystal forming. Experience, further reflection and later learning opportunities all deposit honey in this particular learning hive – your mind.

Of course managers, like military commanders, need to acquire new professional and technical knowledge as they move from team to operational and strategic responsibilities, and these acquisitions properly fall within the broadest spectrum of leadership (role) development. Remember the situational approach – that key part that knowledge plays in the authority of an effective leader at any level? Indeed professional/technical know-how will tend to dominate leadership (role) training at operational level. By then leadership (attribute) should be taken for granted and merely stirred up or refreshed or revisited in ways which I shall explore with you later.

But never fall into the muddle of equating leadership and management development. In the NHS case study, for example, I hope you picked up that only 3 per cent of the employees are managers. Your strategy there had to include *medical leaders* – clinicians, doctors, therapists, nurses. What you were not going to do, I trust, was try to turn these professionals into managers.

It is difficult at first to think in this rather sophisticated way about leadership, but once you get the tune it is easy to remember it. Remember that the actual nomenclature does not really matter. It is not about the semantics of names, more about clarity of concepts. As the Chinese proverb puts it, *It does not matter if a cat is black or white so long as it catches mice*.

CHECKLIST

A STRATEGY FOR LEADERSHIP DEVELOPMENT

Which of these statements would you say applies to your organisation?

There is a clear strategy for the direction of the business. This plan includes a sub-strategy for selecting and developing the right people needed to make the strategy happen. ☐

People frequently comment on lack of a sense of direction and not knowing what the strategy is. ☐

This business does not look ahead more than 12 months. It is pragmatic and driven by short-term results. ☐

	YES	NO
Does your organisation have a strategy for leadership (role) development written down?	☐	☐
Have you seen it?	☐	☐
Does it reflect a clear understanding of such terms as leadership, management and command?	☐	☐
Does your chief executive show ownership of the problem of developing leadership at all levels?	☐	☐

How would you rate your own skills as a strategic thinker?

Good ☐   Average ☐   Weak ☐

▊ KEY POINTS

- What is strategically desirable is not always technically feasible. Usually it is not shortage of money or equipment, but the calibre and knowledge of managers that limits what can be done.

- To build up the strategic capability of an enterprise – its capacity to grow and change, to move forwards along planned lines – you must upgrade the professional and technical capability of its people.

- Good leaders do not fall out of the sky. Wise organisations pay careful heed to selecting and training their leaders, for an essential factor in success is the quality of leadership shown at every level in the enterprise.

- Strategy should not be confused with given tactics, such as running a particular programme for a cohort of senior managers. It always has more than one element in it.

- You can develop leaders in an organisation up to a certain point without the commitment of the board, but beyond that point the exercise is doomed to frustration and failure.

- It is the responsibility of the personnel or 'human resources' director to persuade his/her line colleagues that they are accountable for the third circle – 'developing the individual' – in the context of the common strategy and the evolving organisation.

- Leaders beget leaders. Once the natural system of leadership development takes shape, it then becomes a matter of keeping leadership in good repair.

> "There is an English proverb that says, 'There are no bad students, only bad teachers.' I believe it also applies to a company. There are no bad employees, only bad managers."
>
> T. S. Lin, Chairman of Taiwan's Tatung Co.

5 ■ SELECTION

> "A man with no aptitude for leadership in any direction, either good or bad."
> Plutarch, on Gaius Antonius, a Roman politician

Even the best gardener cannot turn a tulip into a rose, but a good horticulturist can take a tulip and develop a better one. Selection – choosing people with the potential for leadership – is the next key principle to be considered.

Individuals vary in their potential for leadership – the ability to enable a group to achieve its task, to build or maintain it as a team, and to motivate, inspire and develop each person in it. Some have a naturally high aptitude for leadership and others a very low aptitude. You cannot take the latter and turn them into the former. Most managers – or would-be managers – fall somewhere in the middle range of the continuum. Any organisation that means business must ensure that it gains its fair share of potential leaders. In short, it needs a method of selecting men and women with potential as leaders.

◻ THE RIGHT PERSON FOR THE RIGHT JOB

That general description of selection breaks down into two parts:

- The selecting of new young employees from outside the organisation. Some of these may be applying directly for management jobs. Others, seeking specialist appointments in the first instance, may blossom into managers later. Many of these appointments will be made from the ranks of graduates looking for their first job in industry, commerce or the public services.

- Selecting from those applying for promotion to leadership-role appointments, such as heading up a division or department at operational level, or a strategic leadership office such as chief executive. It is not always easy to judge whether or not a person who has shown leadership at one level is capable of exercising leadership at the next level. Many a manager is still promoted to the level of his or her incompetence.

It is worth pausing to reflect upon the amount of money that organisations waste each year by appointing people to business leadership roles who then outdo Gaius Antonius is revealing their total lack of leadership aptitude. They are out of their depth. Just calculate the price-tag of severance settlements, 'head hunter' bills for finding a successor, and of the costs of internal disruption and low morale.

Case study: The unwise university

Once I was invited to speak at a new technological university. At dinner I sat next to the first vice-chancellor, who was soon to retire.

'What are they looking for in your successor?' I inquired.

'There is just one essential requirement,' he replied. 'He should be a Fellow of the Royal Society.'

In due course of time a biochemist with FRS after his name was appointed, one devoid of any leadership aptitude. The appointments board was appraised of his divisive temperament and appalling record with people, but he was the only FRS in sight and so all that was ignored. The university in question endured a decade or more under this abrasive and domineering bully. Two attempts by the governing council to remove him failed on legal grounds. 'Why did they ever appoint him in the first place?' they asked.

▊ SELECTING TEAM LEADERS

The model for successfully assessing leadership potential was first developed by the British Army in the Second World War. The immediate cause was the failure of one-to-one interviewing in choosing the right people to be commissioned. Given the scale of applicants and the need to avoid wasting time and money on those who proved to be unsuitable, something had to be done.

In May 1942 the adjutant general of the day, Sir Ronald Adam, assembled a working party of senior officers and psychologists, including the distinguished Australian social psychiatrist W. R. Bion, who had won a DSO in the First World War. Together they developed a new method of selecting leaders, called in those days the War Office Selection Board (WOSB). It was the grandparent of all later assessment centres.

Candidates for commission attending a three-day WOSB were given a large number to wear. The selectors did not know their names, schools or social backgrounds. Various aptitude tests, role plays, giving a talk, leading a group discussion and an assault course were all fitted into the three days. The pace and demands of the programme introduced an element of stress, no bad thing it was believed when selecting leaders for battle.

The most characteristic and long-enduring element of WOSB was the 'leaderless group' or 'stress group task'. In essence the idea was simple: eight candidates without an appointed leader were given a series of tasks to perform while two observers stood watching and recording what each member did to help achieve the task – getting a barrel over a scaffold obstacle, for example – and to maintain the group as a working unity. In other words a two-factor theory – that there are two poles in a working group, of *task* and *group relation* – had been developed so far as to see the role of a leader as essentially a functional one in relation to these twin ends.

What the candidates were being tested in was the generic role of leader. The elements of the functional leadership general theory were there in the WOSB approach, but in a disconnected and unintegrated way. They did not have, for instance, the actual three-circles model that I had available for training purposes at Sandhurst in the 1960s. Still, it was comparable to the first jet engine, radar or computers – all products of the war; nothing like we have today but nonetheless quantum steps forwards.

WOSBs were introduced for a specific purpose in a given historical context. Although all three British Armed Services continue to employ the method, other organisations – even large ones – have to choose elements from the approach to suit their needs. Comparatively few new entrants or graduates recruited to most organisations will remain in their jobs for more than a few years, yet it is the case that those few may progress from team to operational leadership offices, and maybe – with time away in other organisations – return in strategic leadership roles.

Personally, I should not like to appoint someone to be a team leader without seeing him or her in a group situation with a task to do. That, together with two or three independent interviewers who are or have been successful team leaders in that field, CV and references, should give sufficient grounds for a judgement.

ARE THERE ANY PSYCHOLOGICAL TESTS FOR LEADERSHIP?

Psychological tests fall into two main categories: those testing mental abilities such as the general IQ and specific abilities or aptitudes, and personality/interest questionnaires designed to yield data about the temperament, disposition and attitudes of the candidate.

Cognitive tests have a useful part to play in checking suitability for a range of occupations, as already mentioned. The evidence about personality tests is much more in dispute. In the context of leadership, I know of no questionnaire-type personality test that has any established validity as an indicator of leadership potential or performance.

Such is my own judgement. You will find a confirmation of it with specific reference only to leadership in Lanyon and Goodstein's *Personality assessment* (1997). Incidentally, the authors comment that the claims for 'emotional intelligence' are unsubstantiated. Although constructs such as 'transformational leadership' and 'emotional intelligence' will always enjoy a popular vogue, they have no lasting contribution to leadership assessment.

In other words, if leadership is essentially about doing, then the best way to assess it is to put candidates in simulated or actual situations where they are called upon to act in functionally observable ways, that is, in a group with a group task to perform.

Knowledge, or technical ability and fitness for a particular characteristic working situation, is comparatively easily assessed by those in that particular field. As for *qualities*, I agree with the psychologists' conclusion: 'Traits cannot be directly observed, but must be inferred from patterns of behaviour and experience that are known to be valid trait indicators' (Matthews *et al* 2003).

SELECTING OPERATIONAL BUSINESS LEADERS

It is easy to find a thousand soldiers but hard to find a general, says a Chinese proverb. It is comparatively easy to identify potentially good team leaders, harder to spot operational leaders of real potential, and hardest of all to judge whether or not someone has the makings of excellence as a strategic leader. As Tacitus wrote of Galba, 'Nobody doubted his capacity to rule until he became Emperor.'

As a general principle only those who have proved themselves as team leaders should be considered as operational leaders, and only those who have had sustained success as operational leaders should be chosen as strategic leaders. But there is still a margin where judgement is required. For there is a quantum step between each of the levels, however disguised it may be by the substeps and graduations of rank that large hierarchical organisations use sometimes to 'gear change' the transition.

Unfortunately judgement of people is at present unteachable. Poor judgement of character is often an Achilles' heel of otherwise very good leaders. If that is your weak spot, always employ wise men and women – especially one or two who are accurately intuitive – in your selection of operational leaders. Collective thinking – listening to views and advice – is always a wise policy in judging others: it is a form of collecting information. People decisions are best taken slowly. If there is a rush or a panic to appoint at this level, you have come down the wrong road.

SELECTION IN PERSPECTIVE

I look upon leadership selection – choosing the right person in the first place – as half the battle won. There is an old gypsy saying that you make your profit when you buy the goods. I once asked Dmitri Comino, a successful entrepreneur and industrialist, for his secrets of motivating people. 'John, it is very difficult to motivate people; it makes a lot more sense to employ people who are motivated already.'

Those words apply to leadership too. It is very hard to make people into leaders. Why not choose people who have the seeds or sparks of leadership in them already? Leadership *development* – from the French word 'to unwrap' – implies that there is something there to unfold. Make sure there is potential there – high-grade ore, not 'fool's gold' or low-grade rock – before you buy the goods.

Always encourage people to put themselves forwards for leadership roles. It is a sign of corporate health and high morale if the people are eager to take on leadership responsibility. A volunteer is always better than a pressed man. If such a person is not selected he or she needs to be given the reasons, and left with no sense of diminished self-esteem.

The identification of the three-circles practical philosophy – the generic role of leader – greatly simplifies the task of selection. Potential for it at *team* level, for example, can be explored under these six question headings:

Qualities

- Has this person the kind of qualities which exemplify those expected in the team he or she will lead?

- Does he or she display at least in embryo the generic qualities of enthusiasm, integrity and openness to learn?

Context

- Does this person have the intellectual capability to acquire the necessary knowledge and practical experience necessary to command respect?

- Is there evidence that he or she has the interests, aptitudes and temperament appropriate to this field of work?

Group

- Has there been any track record of team leadership in any field – work, social, family, school, sport, hobbies?

- Is the potential there for enabling a group to achieve its task, building or maintaining it as a team, and motivating individuals?

Lastly, humility or lack of arrogance is a leadership quality that those selecting people for leadership positions need to bear in mind. I heard Montgomery, in a talk to 800 officer cadets at Sandhurst on the subject of leadership, tell a story which stuck in my mind as an object lesson in humility:

> **"**One day my company commander called me into his office and said, 'Montgomery, I have been watching you very carefully and you will never rise above the rank of major.'
>
> 'Well,' said the Field Marshal to the assembled rows of officer cadets with a twinkle in his eye, 'well, gentlemen, he was wrong. It was he who never rose above the rank of major!'**"**

CHECKLIST

SELECTION

	YES	NO
Does your organisation specifically attempt to assess leadership potential at all levels of managerial appointments?	☐	☐
Does the framework you use employ the generic role of *leader* concept?	☐	☐
Have you ever rejected a professional qualified or technically competent candidate on any of the following grounds:	☐	☐
■ Would be no team leader.	☐	☐
■ A substantial doubt about personal or professional integrity.	☐	☐
■ Racial, gender or sexual orientation prejudice.	☐	☐
Setting aside the hyperbole word 'passion', does your organisation always look for enthusiasm and commitment in its leaders-to-be?	☐	☐

Write down the names of five persons that you have appointed as leaders in the last two years. In terms of effective leadership, how do they look now?

1 Poor   2 Average   3 Good   4 Very Good   5 Excellent

....

....

....

....

....

If you score less than 15, reread this chapter immediately.

▐ KEY POINTS

- ■ An accurate assessment of leadership potential – a prediction of probable performance in terms of the task, team and individual – comes from placing people in working groups and seeing what they do.

- ■ Such a group approach to leadership selection should be the core of the initial selection process for those aspiring to be leaders who have passed the first screening, supported by full biodata, interviews, industry-related tests and psychological tests.

- ■ Selection procedures should be so designed that they enable people to assess their own strengths and weaknesses. People should be encouraged to assess their own suitability for a particular job or field of work.

- ■ Selectors should be chosen carefully from line managers with a proven track record as managers of people at work. Some initial training in selection methods should be given to them.

- ■ The principles of leadership selection should apply to internal appointments. People should be encouraged to apply for promotion and submit themselves to a selection committee or board which is fair and seen to be fair.

- ■ Humility is important in selectors. It is an ingredient of practical wisdom that keeps one open to learning the lessons from one's mistakes. For nobody gets it right every time.

- ■ Remember that all you are doing in selection is to identify potential – especially at the younger end of the age continuum. Your organisation now has the challenge – both in its corporate interest and also for the benefit of the individual concerned – to develop that potential. Do it in partnership together.

> **"**It is important for everyone to believe, whether they succeed or not, that success is linked with some kind of logic and beholden to some notion of legitimacy .... To put it another way, it is psychologically intolerable, having risen to the heights, to be badgered by doubt that you do not really deserve it.**"**
>
> Alistair Mant

6 ▪ TRAINING FOR LEADERSHIP

"Training is everything. The peach was once a bitter almond; cauliflower is nothing but cabbage with a college education."

Mark Twain *Pudd'nhead Wilson* 1894

An selection procedure, however good, will only identify and to some extent measure a person's natural (including acquired) *potential* for leadership. That potential has to be developed. Leadership training has the key part to play in that process. The strongest and most relevant expression of this third principle to your organisation is in this axiom: *Your organisation should never give anyone a team leadership role without giving the person concerned appropriate leadership training for it.*

For me this axiom has an almost moral force. For me it is simply morally wrong – a failure in trust – to ignore it. We do not entrust our children to bus drivers, train drivers, teachers or doctors who have had no training. Why do we entrust our valued personnel to team leaders who have had no training in leadership? It is wrong for the people concerned; it is wrong, too, for the leader in question. For 80 per cent of poor leaders are poor only because no one explained to them what leadership is and encouraged them to become leaders. And whose fault is that?

Without the three-circles breakthrough, then, training for leadership was a bridge too far. That was my position in the 1960s, and that is still my position today some 40 years later. I have taught nothing but the generic leadership role. When Socrates was asked why he repeated his core teaching so much instead of moving on to new things –the Greeks were the first to hold the modern heresy that newer is truer – he replied, 'If I am asked what two plus two makes, shall I not reply four?'

THE PRIORITY OF TEAM LEADERSHIP TRAINING

Several times I have referred to the global surge of interest in, and use of, the words 'leader' and 'leadership'. It is sometimes called the leadership movement, leadership industry or leadership revolution. Behind the ever-spreading popular truism that old-style command and control management has had its day and we are now in the age of leadership, there is an element of truth. The real revolution was an intellectual or conceptual one, like the discovery of DNA; it took place in the 1960s and yet its significance has remained hidden to all but a few – until this book. It was the discovery of the generic role of *leader* and the three-circles understanding of leadership as both role and attribute that sprang from it, I have suggested, that was the golden key.

At once a locked door opened. For centuries the maxim 'leaders are born, not made' had reigned unchallenged. There had been no serious attempt to teach leadership since the days of Socrates, beyond inflicting young people with discourses on the virtues or qualities of leaders. Now, at least in theory, it suddenly became possible to train leaders. Experiments with some 5,000 officer cadets at Sandhurst soon turned that theory into daily practice. Getting to the moon had once seemed impossible; now we knew it could be done.

After I began by writing the world's first book on the subject, I have always been primarily interested in the practical business of *leadership development*. But that subject has been largely ignored by the leadership industry. Another major contrast between the Leadership Industry and myself is that I have always stressed the priority of training for team leadership (while not neglecting work at operational and strategic levels of leadership – on the thesis that success depends upon excellence at all three levels and teamwork between them).

The leadership industry, true to its largely American origins, has been obsessed with attempting to develop 'transformational leadership' at the higher-operational/strategic end of the spectrum. The report of the Council for Excellence in Management and Leadership on best-practice leadership development (2001) revealed the all too common unconscious assumption that leaders are simply those at or near the top of an organisation. Most of the services and products of the leadership industry – business schools, large and small management consultancies, as well as extensive and expensive in-house programmes – have been directed at this segment of the market. It is what could be called low volume and high profit.

My quest has been a different one. Take, for example, the 386,400 nurses in the National Health Service (p49). By rule of thumb, 39,000 of them will be team leaders (whatever the nomenclature). Let's assume they are in that role for three years on average. That means we have 13,000 nurse team leaders *a year* to train. That is more than the total number of police sergeants (leaders of ten police officers) in the United Kingdom Here what we need is high-volume, high-quality and low-cost training.

Let me explain why I say that. The implication of $e = mc^2$, as we all know, is that an immense amount of energy can be extracted from a tiny amount of matter – hence atomic energy. On that analogy, the discovery of the generic role of leader meant that theoretically we could extract powerful learning from a very small compass of time – one and a half or two (residential) days, to be precise. The design of an atomic bomb took the time and brains of thousands of scientists working over years in the Manhattan Project, but eventually the theoretical possibility implicit in $e = mc^2$ became a reality. In my field of leadership development it took some three years, with the help of a few exceptional colleagues, to design the one-and-a-half day programme which would fully release the power of the three-circles model.

Don't forget that in 10 to 15 years' time globally we need to be training about one million team leaders *annually*. Thanks to the three-circles breakthrough, believe it or not, it is feasible to do that. Technically feasible, I mean, for whether or not the political will to do it emerges remains to be seen. We pay a heavy price for neglecting the development of leadership – good leadership and leadership for good – in tomorrow's political leaders.

THE HALLMARKS OF HIGH-VOLUME, HIGH-QUALITY AND LOW-COST TEAM LEADERSHIP TRAINING

To return to my metaphor of the laws of aerodynamics, how do we design an effective course with those characteristics? I suggest that you should always look for the following hallmarks:

- **Simple:** the content of the course should be simple. It should concentrate on what *must* be learnt, as opposed to the *should* and *might* areas. There should be a lack of unnecessary complications and management or psychological jargon.

- **Practical:** the approach should be essentially practical, focusing on the actions of leadership. There should be no abstractions or theory for its own sake.

- **Participative:** when people are talking they are thinking; they learn by doing and reviewing what they have done in the light of the principles of leadership.

- **Variety:** case studies, indoor and outdoor exercises, small group discussions, plenary sessions, lectures on key points, films or videos, and individual checklists all create variety. Keep them guessing what is coming next.

- **Enjoyable:** the enjoyability of a course is important, because if it isn't enjoyable adults will learn but little. But if it's *only* enjoyable that's tantamount to failure.

- **Relevant:** if neither the participants nor the trainer can see any relevance to the actual job of leading that they are doing, or shortly will be doing, it's unlikely the course will be effective.

- **Short:** about two or three days is right for most leadership courses at all levels. Beyond that the programme is in danger of becoming repetitive or academic. *Less is more.*

You will have guessed by now what I think the content of the course should be. But it is not fixed in concrete. One day someone will produce a better, simpler, clearer, more comprehensive concept of leadership. Humanity doesn't stand still, but it hasn't happened yet. Until it does – unless you have unlimited time and money to waste – don't try to reinvent the wheel. We know what leadership is and how to train for it. Use that knowledge, but adapt it to your context or situation.

The functional leadership/ACL course

Day 1

Session

1	9.30	**Introduction:**
		Course objective and definition of need for leadership
	9.55	**Group discussion**
	10.30	**Report back** – discuss
	10.45	**The qualities, situational and functional approach to leadership**
2	12.00	**Observations and discussion**
		Practice in observing leadership
3	12.15	**Sharing decisions**
	12.45	(approx.) Lunch

4	2.00	**Leadership exercise II**
		Observation and discussion
5	2.45	**Motivation**
6	3.30	**Leadership film** – Part 1 Analysis and discussion
		Practice in identifying and observing leadership

Day 2

Session

7	9.45	Part II
	10.45	Analysis and discussion
		Practice in identifying and observing leadership
8	11.30	**Leadership exercise III**
		Analysis and discussion
		Further practice in observing leadership
9	12.15	**Practical implications of the model**
	12.45	(approx.) Lunch
10	2.00	**An organisational case study**
		Practical implications applied
11	3.00	Reporting back on organisational case study
12	3.45	Discussion of group reporting back action following the course
	4.45	Course conclusion

THE AUXILIARY ROLE OF E-LEARNING

The advent of e-learning seemed to herald the end of training courses and the era of individual self-development – individuals sitting in front of a screen and teaching themselves through interactive computer programs. The Internet, of course, is an amazing technological revolution that will affect every domain of training and education.

In the leadership development field, given the interpersonal and skill-related nature of the subject, there is no substitute for face-to-face learning and practice. Yet if the essentials of the *must know* have to be conveyed in that context, e-learning can come into its own in the following phase: filling out the background and outline of the *must know*, and beginning to paint in the *should know* and *could know* inner and outer rings of the learning priority circle (see Figure 6.1).

Figure 6.1 The learning priority circle

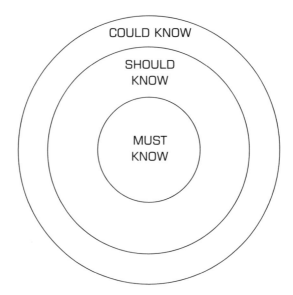

Obviously the further away one moves from the core, the greater the number of options or choices that should be open to the student. In part, personal profiling of strengths and weaknesses will help to guide students in their choices.

What is the possible content of the *should know* and *could know* domains? The latest speculative or esoteric theories, fads or fashions of leadership? Not for my money. I should be looking more towards the 'neighbour concepts' of leadership, the inhabitants in the other houses in the street named 'the human side of enterprise'.

The e-learning programmes I have so far seen on leadership are marked by ignorance of the body of knowledge that exists on the subject, poor design and lack of imagination, with little attempt made to use the technology to engage or help the student.

It is paper-based distance learning, lecture notes and handouts, lacking in intellectual credibility. Some people just download these courses and read them on the commuter train – e-reading rather than e-learning.

Going back to my nursing example, if you have 13,000 new team leaders a year you can afford to invest a lot of money to get the world's best *must, should* and *could* follow-up to the two-day functional leadership course. That is always providing, of course, that you can persuade 350 trusts, 28 regional strategic authorities and professional bodies such as the Royal College of Nursing to transcend their own interests and put the whole before the parts. It is a good example of the need for strategic leadership in the field of leadership development.

OUTDOOR LEADERSHIP TRAINING FOR MANAGERS

This outdoor training – often now called *experiential* – was a direct product of the field leadership training I initiated at Sandhurst and described in Chapter 6 of *Training for leadership* (Adair 1968). For its early history and a case study from the United States of the use of the three-circles model in that context, see Appendix 5 of that book.

On the basis of my pioneering work in this respect a new field opened up, and there are now many organisations operating globally as providers. John Storey in *Leadership in organisations* (2004) provides a context here in his useful overview of the burgeoning field:

> "Experiential learning and simulation. This mode of provision is very popular. It usually takes place in mountainous locales or in close proximity to the sea and small boats. Courses of this type operate on the basis of action learning or learning by doing. The work of John Adair (1983) often provides the basic underlying framework. The residential courses offering this approach are built around a series of outdoor tasks and challenges. The trainers act as facilitators and feed back information about behaviour patterns; from these, participants embark on a journey of self-discovery."

Just to be clear, I would not classify the functional leadership/ACL course as outdoor, though it is certainly experiential. There are three kinds of 'substitute group tasks': tabletop exercises (such as constructing things with Lego bricks); outdoor 'command tasks' in the grounds (such as getting a barrel over some scaffolding); and use of the natural environment for extended or composite group exercises. Functional leadership/ ACL employs the first and/or second, but usually not the third.

The central issue in all outdoor leadership and teamwork training using the natural environment is always *transfer*. It may be enjoyable to learn sailing, abseiling or canoeing but where is the pay-off? What is the relevance of these skills or activities to back-home work? The answer, of course, is that in themselves they are not transferable. But they are vehicles for exploring the generic role of leader and the related process skills of decision-making, problem-solving, creative thinking, communication – speaking, listening, meetings, and both self-control and time management.

▌ THE OTHER TWO LEVELS OF LEADERSHIP

At these levels 'training' is not really the proper word: we are talking in more general terms (in the context of courses, programmes, seminars, master classes) here about a practically oriented form of education.

Tentatively – very tentatively – I hold the hypothesis that there is a natural 'window of opportunity' for acquiring the three-circles practical philosophy. It is somewhere between school/university and one's first or second year as a team leader at work. Miss that opportunity and you never lay down a foundation on which to build your own walls and roof. To anyone who has studied learning, what I am saying will sound blindingly obvious. As the Bedouin proverb says, *Learning in old age is writing on sand, but learning in youth is engraving on rock.* In other words, many people miss the boat, and remedial programmes in later life – in my experience – never quite make up for it. When a manager is, say, 41 or 42 it is a bit late to have to say to him or her, 'By the way, there is this thing called leadership …'.

The principle that heads this chapter, however, still applies. Somehow or other you have to convey what is expected of a person occupying an operational leadership role in your organisation. Remember that expectations determine role, and we do know what the generic role of leader is *at all levels*. Even if, at rock-bottom worst, you do no more than hand a newly-appointed operational leader your current list of 84 leadership competencies, you must say something to him or her, so that the *organisation's* expectation is crystal clear. External courses or programmes are always supplementary to these internal briefings or seminars, at which the chief executive is the principal teacher – see Principle 7 (Chapter 10).

Speaking of the chief executive, he or she is the one person who your organisation cannot train, educate or induct as a strategic leader – at least not in any formal sense. Yet the chief executive is a keystone of the whole arch of leadership development. What can be done? Here we have recently made an important breakthrough, which again I shall describe and discuss under Principle 7 in Chapter 10.

CHECKLIST

TRAINING FOR LEADERSHIP

Interpreting 'team leadership level' in its broadest sense, does your organisation apply the principle that no team leader should be given the office without two-days-plus leadership training?

Completely   7   6   5   4   3   2   1   Not at all

If you have circled a rating of 1, 2, 3 or 4 please give the reasons (not excuses) that this is the case:

If you have circled a rating of 5, 6 or 7, write down what you intend to do to improve the programme:

Are all operational leaders in your organisation up to executive director level clear about the generic role of leader, its functions, qualities and knowledge requirements?

All ☐   Many ☐   Some ☐   None ☐

Did they acquire that understanding of the role and proficiency in spite of the organisation or because of it?

In spite of ☐   Because of ☐

Have you the moral courage to show this completed checklist to your chief executive?

Yes ☐   No ☐   Will sleep on it ☐

KEY POINTS

- Courses in leadership – formal or informal training – constitute only a small part in the formation of a leader. But it is important to get this training element right.

- The path to successful courses lies in the seven hallmarks: simple, practical, participative, variety, enjoyable, relevant and short.

- The sovereign principle is to keep it simple. That doesn't mean being simplistic or superficial. As Einstein once said, 'Everything should be made as simple as possible, but not simpler.'

- Leadership training, like leadership itself, should be fun. There is no excuse for being boring or dull about what is, after all, one of the most fascinating and mysterious subjects in the world.

- According to the well-known 'Peter Principle', leaders are often promoted to the level of their incompetence. That may be the result of a faulty or inadequate internal promotion system. Or it may be because your organisation has failed to provide these leaders with an opportunity to stand back, reflect and review again the principles of leadership in the context of what lies immediately ahead.

- Good leadership training also equips people to be more effective in the other two principal roles in organisations: subordinate and colleague, or – if you prefer it – team member.

- Leadership is learnt principally by experience and practice. Ideas and principles can help to prepare people for leadership roles and to cut down the time and/or cost of learning on the job. Courses are the best way of introducing those principles in a way that influences subsequent performance.

"A good beginning makes a good ending."
English proverb

7 ■ A CAREER DEVELOPMENT POLICY

"There is a tide in the affairs of men
Which, taken at the flood, leads on to fortune;
Omitted, all the voyage of their life
Is bound in shallows and in miseries."
William Shakespeare *Julius Caesar* 1599

You know the old story about an absent-minded professor who gave his young son lectures on the theory of cycling, complete with coloured slides of his own cycling holidays in the Alps. He inspired the boy to want to ride, but some reason or other, never got around to giving him a bike. In the context of leadership development; you need to provide the bike.

Leadership is always learnt on the job, by practice. All else is auxiliary. The pearl of great price that an organisation can give to a person who wants to develop as a leader is simple – the opportunity to lead. The governing principle is:

"Give the right opportunity to the right person at the right time in order
to develop his or her abilities – for the benefit of both the organisation and
the individual."

It is important that those responsible for leadership development should have a systematic approach to career planning in their organisations. It helps to think about the fundamental nature of careers.

ON CAREERS

The word 'career' is now used so frequently to describe a person's progress in life, or by derivation from this his or her profession or vocation, that it is difficult to recall that it once meant a racecourse and a gallop – hence the phrase 'careering about'.

The origin of 'career' is the Latin word for carriage road. It came to be used for racecourse, gallop, and by extension any rapid and unrestrained activity. It was applied first to the advancement of diplomats and politicians, and then to indicate progress in a vocation, and finally the vocation itself. Nowadays it is used about all jobs that have some implicit promise of progress, but most widely for jobs with explicit internal development – 'a career in the Civil Service'. 'Career' now usually suggests continuity, if not necessarily promotion or advancement.

The distinction between a *career* and a *job* only partly depends upon this implication of progress and development, for it is associated also with some class distinctions between different sorts of work. Does a carpenter or a miner have a career or job? The extension of the term, as in 'careers advice', somewhat dilutes these associations, but they cling on obstinately in the form of hidden assumptions. The same class overtones cast their long shadow on the distinction between 'development' and 'training' – the former is thought fitting to managers and the latter held to be suitable for use about workers or young people. In fact it is usually managers who need training while everyone else needs development!

It is interesting that the early use of 'career' carried a derogatory sense of being unrestrained in one's progress upwards or onwards. That is still present in the words 'careerism' and 'careerist' – one who advances his or her career, often at the cost of integrity.

Another derogatory note is struck when people refer to their career as a rat race, by which they mean they experience it as a violent, senseless and usually competitive activity or rush. It is a phrase that vividly recalls the original metaphor or the racecourse. Perhaps managerial careers become rat races for their owners if there is no training, no planning, and no sense of purpose.

The very concept of a career suggests that there is some explicit internal development, some progress or advancement. It is natural that those who embark upon a career should want to move up the ladder as high as they can. That does not imply that they are all careerists, although you will always find a few in every walk of life. The steps on the ladder are promotions to bigger and more important jobs, usually signposted as such by the salary that goes with them. In the context of developing leadership, each significant step will normally involve a larger responsibility for people. It should also take you onto the higher and steeper slopes, where the challenge of leadership is greatest: the risks of failure are more awesome and the rewards of success are correspondingly greater.

The more people share in decisions that affect their working lives, the more motivated they are to carry them out. It would be foolish not to apply that principle in the field of career development.

Granted that an organisation or an industry (in the widest sense) has able people who are keen to have a career when it comes to steps on the ladder – or even choices between ladders – then it needs to work out a system to ensure that people come up to the senior roles of operational and strategic leadership with the right experience and training behind them. How does an organisation do that?

THE HOURGLASS MODEL OF CAREER CHANGE

The hourglass model of career change which I first developed in the 1980s throws some more light on levels of leadership. Some people in organisations, I suggest, follow career paths that resemble an inverted funnel. They begin broad-based at school, choose between arts and sciences (too soon in Britain, many argue), then specialise still further. The process is repeated or continued at university and in postgraduate training, especially in the science-based and vocationally orientated courses. Again the process is repeated or refined further when a person enters employment: he or she is – or will soon become – a specialist. In some fields – music, science or medicine are examples – it is possible for such a person to progress to the top, in terms of salary and status, while remaining essentially an individual contributor. It is a bad feature of British business in the past – and parts of it today – that specialists such as engineers, scientists, accountants or salespeople could only be promoted by being made managers and put in charge of others. For many specialists such promotion is as unwelcome to them as it is unfair to those who must work for them.

For many other specialists, however, becoming a manager fits in with their career plans. Their potential for 'getting results through people' may have been evident to them for a long time, or it may have been first identified in the selection process of the organisation in question. Whichever way, they *want* to be managers or leaders.

At that point in their careers they are moving through the narrow neck of the hourglass – it may have been long or short in their cases – and are becoming generalists again.

Figure 7.1 The hourglass model of career change

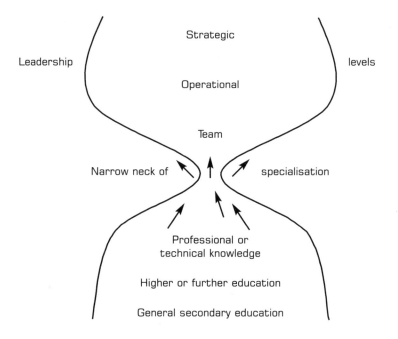

The degree to which they will retain a specialist contribution to the output of the organisation clearly varies from situation to situation. But the pattern has been altered: the new generalist role should set the tone.

Three 'widening' processes need to occur if people emerging from the narrow neck are to advance eventually to a strategic leadership role.

- Their knowledge of the enterprise as a whole – finance and marketing, production and distribution in the case of industry – needs to be developed and consolidated, partly by training but mainly by experience of managing or working in more than one area of the organisation's operations.

- They need to develop in the generic role of leader, understanding what is required first at operational and then at strategic level. That encompasses both the intellectual skills of strategic thinking and the human skills of taking colleagues with you on the journey.

- They need time management skills. If you cannot delegate and plan your time you will lack time to think, time for people, time for allies, partners, key customers and any form of social responsibility.

The hourglass model is extremely useful in helping individuals to think about the direction of their careers. It shouldn't be pressed too far: a leading heart surgeon is certainly a team leader, and may also be a contributor at operational and strategic levels. Those who have chosen the generalist path may well keep their hands in as specialists. I can think of one vice-chancellor, a biochemist by profession, who spends a half-day a week working as a team member in a research team led by a young lecturer in the university's biochemistry department.

THE PRINCIPLES OF SUCCESSION PLANNING

There are two basic approaches to career development. One starts with the person and works forward. The other starts with the senior leadership roles and works backwards.

One essential system in most organisations, especially the larger ones, is *succession planning*. Beside each job, especially in the senior management, three or four names of probable, possible or potential successors should be written down. If the present job-holder suddenly resigned through ill health, who would succeed him or her? That name is the *probable* successor.

The *possible* successors should include one or two names of younger managers. Bear in mind that a survey of 200 chief executives revealed that the average age when they entered senior management was 32. They achieved the top job at an average age of 41. On the way up these 'high flyers' had worked in eight or more different jobs in two or three different organisations. Behind these facts we can glimpse an essential story, admittedly speeded up in the case of budding chief executives, but true for all who aspire to rise as leaders in organisations. It is the process by which a specialist becomes a generalist by planned career moves.

The characteristically difficult task facing many organisations is persuading the divisions and companies to release managers in order that they might diversify their experience. The request for a move for a young manager invariably arrives when he or she is in the throes of a uniquely difficult product launch!

Organisations that have decentralized for sound commercial reasons may find more difficulty in arranging such cross-postings. If that is the case they may need to review their attitudes and systems. Alfred Sloan, a great president of General Motors, once wisely said that the central issue in organisation is the relation of the parts to the whole. Getting the balance right is not easy. Like equiposing two scales, once the balance is more or less right what is needed is constant minor adjustments. Within the sum of things, making postings or promotions with the career development needs of the group (whole) as opposed to the division or company (part) in mind is a relatively small matter.

Those same company chief executives who are reluctant to release people may want someone in three or four years' time, possibly as a potential successor. 'I don't want him,' they will say of a suggested name, 'he has only worked in one place.'

Apart from the understandable reluctance of some parts to release people for work in other parts of the organisation for the common good, there are other reasons that potential 'high-flyers' may turn down career development moves. Working wives or husbands who don't want to leave their jobs, children at school who shouldn't be moved at this stage of their education, and the need to be near an ageing parent, are but three of the reasons given.

In an international organisation a refusal to work overseas will obviously limit a manager's career. The refusal to work in different parts of the country for a manager within a national organisation will have the same effect.

Leadership always carries a price tag. At the higher levels the rewards may be indeed greater – I don't mean the material or extrinsic rewards of money, privileges or honours – but the burden is much heavier. Not least for many there is a sense of aloneness. In the English language the words 'lead' and 'load' are etymological cousins. Thus self-selection comes into play: some individuals with aptitude for leadership at operational or strategic levels choose not to put themselves forward.

Nor should organisations put pressure on people to become leaders, still less bribe them into it. It is legitimate to present opportunities and challenges, even to say, 'In our view you are the right person.' But freedom contains the sacred right of rejection. Sometimes wise people instinctively know when they have reached the level at which they can do their best work.

Room at the top

Occasionally, I have heard some young man say cynically that advancement is usually the result of 'getting lucky breaks'. This is a defeatist attitude that I deplore. It would be less than honest to say that good fortune – being there, in the right place, when the lightning strikes – does not play its part. Yet when opportunity comes, even by chance, the man must be prepared, must be able to deliver; otherwise, his triumph will be short-lived. A steady rise to a position of pre-eminence most often comes with hard work, constant effort at self-improvement – and devotion to principle.

One day during my White House years, I called in an assistant – a highly competent man of fine personality – and asked him if he would like to have a more responsible and remunerative job which was then open. I explained that he would be operating rather independently, largely responsible for his own decisions. He thought a moment and then said, 'No, I'd be no good at it. I am a No. 2 man – and I think a good one – but I am not a No. 1 man. I am not fitted for such a job, and I don't want it.'

Although his answer startled me, I respected his honesty. Moreover, this world always needs competent No. 2 men, also good No. 3, No. 4 and No. 5 men – and each, on his own level, can be a good performer.

Yet I would urge any young man with ambition never to be too hasty in concluding that he doesn't have the stature for top leadership. Often I have seen a man who had doubts about his own resources rise to the occasion and perform with great competence when the opportunity finally came.

Dwight D. Eisenhower

Eisenhower (see box) strikes the right balance: encouraging and supporting younger men and women to take on greater leadership responsibilities, but accepting their decision if they decline and maintaining his respect for them.

EQUAL OPPORTUNITIES

Any career development policy must be fair, and seem to be fair. Promotion should be solely on the basis of merit, not on account of favouritism, nepotism or 'political correctness'.

One of the great new facts of our times is that about 50 per cent of leadership roles are now occupied by women. The exception is at strategic leadership level, especially in industry and commerce. How far this fact is a result of residual prejudice – largely unconscious, no doubt – in those responsible for the career development policy, and how far there is an element of self-selection at work, it is hard to say.

"Even when the path is normally open – when there is nothing to prevent a woman from being a doctor, a lawyer, a Civil Servant – there are many phantoms and obstacles, I believe, looming in her way."

Virginia Woolf

Fortunately the leader in the generic role concept is identified only as a *person*. Therefore issues such as gender, nationality, sexual orientation, race or colour, age or ability/disability do not enter into the picture, except in the axiom that leaders tend to exemplify the qualities expected, required or admired in the groups they lead. So if you are an atheist don't apply to be the next Pope.

If your organisation is getting it right it will not allow the leaders of tomorrow to stagnate in jobs. That does not mean they should be moved every year before their mistakes have a chance to catch up on them! There has to be time to achieve some objectives, to build up a track record, but the emphasis should be upon onwards and upwards. That means wider knowledge, gained through working in a ranger of functional areas. It may include secondments and periods away from the organisation altogether. This widening of experience, however, should be coupled with a deepening of the manager's understanding of strategic leadership within the competitive environment and a rapidly changing world.

CHECKLIST

A CAREER DEVELOPMENT POLICY

	YES	NO

Does your organisation have a coherent career development policy, encompassing succession planning for key posts? ☐ ☐

How often does each manager have a session in which he/she can share his/her career directions and learn what the organisation may be able to offer?

Annual ☐   Bi-annual ☐   Every five years ☐   Never ☐

Review the last 10 appointments your organisation made to leadership positions in the broad-band operational level.
How many appointments were made from those outside the organisation?

1   2   3   4   5   6   7   8   9   10

If you have circled any number above 3, would you agree that you either your organisation does not have a career development policy or it is not working very well? ☐ ☐

Are more than 25 per cent of your more senior level of managers women? ☐ ☐

Do you operate a 'fast-track' leadership development programme for those in their twenties and early thirties? ☐ ☐

Is it public knowledge and can anyone apply to be selected for it? ☐ ☐

◼ KEY POINTS

- It is essential for organisations – the chief executive and the principal staff person on the human resources side – to draw up a succession plan for the more important jobs.

- The very word 'career' implies progress or development within a work context. Leadership development in organisations should be integrated closely with the steps an individual takes upon the career ladder.

- Among the names under each job in the succession plan there should be at least one of a person in his or her twenties or early thirties.

- Careers develop either like an hourglass, opening up after a period of narrow-focus specialization, or like a funnel, where people more or less remain in their specialization.

- Large organisations lose one of their advantages if cross-postings for the purposes of management development cannot be made. The parts of a corporate body should never be allowed to become so particular that the interests of the whole are sacrificed on the altar of divisional profits.

- Drawing up succession options shows up vulnerable positions, opens minds to unusual possibilities and engenders a sense that succession is in control

- Career moves should be aimed at developing general capability, not merely at grooming a person for a specific job.

- Involve people as far as possible in decisions about their professional future.

- Ensure that your career development policy – the opportunities part of it – is not only fair but seen to be fair.

> **"**I took a good deal o' pains with his education, sir; let him run the streets when he was very young, and shift for his-self. It's the only way to make a boy sharp, sir.**"**
>
> Charles Dickens, *Pickwick Papers* 1837

8 ■ LINE MANAGERS AS LEADERSHIP MENTORS

"At a crisis in my youth, he taught me the wisdom of choice. To try and fail is at least to learn; to fail to try is to suffer the inestimable loss of what might have been."

Chester Barnard

In the development of a leader of stature one or more mentors have often played a significant part. What is a mentor? The word is derived from Greek mythology. When the hero Odysseus left Ithaca he entrusted his son Telemachus to an old friend on the island named Mentor. The goddess Athena took Mentor's shape on more than one occasion to help Telemachus in the difficulties that befell Ithaca during his father's absence. Under Mentor's inspired tutelage the untried youth eventually became a seasoned leader.

Telemachus appeared at first in the story as a good and dutiful son, but lacking in spark or drive: he was timid and unenterprising. Later, at the behest of Athena working though Mentor, he ordered his mother's domineering suitors to depart. When they refused, guided by Mentor he resolved to sail to the mainland and report the calamitous turn of events to his father. As the story continues Telemachus demonstrates ever more resolve, energy and resourcefulness. When Telemachus eventually joins Odysseus upon the latter's return to Ithaca, he acts as an intelligent and enterprising helper. He astonishes his mother Penelope, for example, by taking command in the house and leading the fight against the over-mighty suitors.

This Greek myth does illustrate a truth about leadership. Leaders are inspiring. In order to become so they need to be inspired themselves. Mentors are those who inspire us with a vision of leadership. They often do it as much by their example as by their words.

I sometimes think, incidentally, that leadership is like a torch handed from one runner in a relay race to another, rather than a subject that can be learnt from a book. It is a matter of the spirit. Some people – very few in my experience – have the power to ignite the fire by the sparks of their words or presence. They may be quite unconscious that they are acting as leadership mentors. Characteristically such mentors have a high opinion of you:

- They perceive more within you than you can see yourself.

- They encourage you to set demanding goals and aspire to high standards of conduct, both professional and personal.

- At times they seem to expect or require a great deal from you, more than you feel capable of delivering.

- But their example and their support proves to be decisive and you rise to meet the challenge.

CAN MENTORING BE DEVELOPED?

A review of my own experience makes me initially doubtful whether mentoring – as it has been called – can ever be organised or systematised. It is the natural inclination of managers to turn everything into systems, as I have already suggested. It would be convenient and nice if everyone in a hierarchical organisation was a mentor to the 10 or 12 people who report to him or her. But it is not as simple as that. To send out an e-mail to all managers directing them to become 'leadership mentors' is unlikely to be effective. Behind many managers there are such mentors in their early careers.

Andrew Carnegie owed much to his senior, Thomas A. Scott. As head of the Western Division of the Pennsylvania Railroad, Scott recognised talent and the desire to learn in the young telegrapher assigned to him. By giving Carnegie increasing responsibility and by providing him with the opportunity to learn through close personal observation, Scott added to Carnegie's self-confidence and sense of achievement. Because of his own personal strength and achievement, Scott did not fear Carnegie's aggressiveness. Rather, he gave it full play in encouraging Carnegie's initiative.

Could line managers be trained to do this? A proliferation of courses in coaching, counselling and appraisal suggests they can.

Going back to the three-circles model, a part of the leadership strategy in all organisations should be to persuade all line managers that they are essentially leaders, and therefore that they own part of the third circle – developing the individual – simply because it is a key part of their role, what they are paid to do.

The levels at which they operate in that third area will vary considerably. On the swimming analogy, almost everyone can be taught to swim but few will ever reach the highest level of Olympic performance.

DEVELOPING THE INDIVIDUAL

Line managers who see the three-circles model as defining the essence of their role will naturally welcome and accept their responsibility for developing leadership potential. That involves far more than just sending the person concerned on a course. It means trying to do 'on the job' leadership training. That involves applying the function of evaluating in the form of appraising the individual – identifying strengths and weaknesses, encouraging, advising and listening. An annual appraisal interview should be viewed as simply the annual stock-take. It is both the summation of all the informal reviews during the year and the time when the balance sheet of the year's performance is reviewed, but it is far from being the natural and everyday learning process I have in mind.

Before and after a person goes on a leadership course it should be a standard process that he or she should be briefed and debriefed by the person he or she reports to. The talk prior to the course is to establish clearly why the organisation thinks it worth spending its money and the time of the individual on the course. The person's training needs and the course objectives have to tie up. Afterwards the line manager will want to know what the course member has identified as action points, so that he or she can help in implementing them. The course may have suggested changes in the way the department or section is organised or run, which will need digesting – sometimes with a strong drink!

If your line managers are themselves leaders of some stature, leading by example as well as precept, the young managers will be learning a great deal more from working with them, observing them and talking to them than they can ever put into words. If that is happening, they are well on their way to becoming leadership mentors.

To be realistic, however, up until quite recent times, some line managers plainly lacked the necessary leadership qualities – not to mention the inspiration of Athena – to act as mentors in developing leaders. One attempt to make up the deficiency was for the chief executive to appoint as mentors, or 'godfathers' and 'godmothers', some senior managers who do not have line responsibility for the young manager. Some organisations still follow this route with good effect, especially with graduate recruits.

Another remedy was to invite a young manager to choose his or her own mentor within the organisation, not unlike selecting a father-confessor. This method worked well in some contexts. For example, I know one head of a university department who decided to follow this course after attending a leadership course. Upon her return to the university she approached another head – a wise person – to act as her mentor in matters of leadership and management. Both have enjoyed and benefited from the relationship.

Mentoring or coaching as a professional management consultancy service is well established. There are plenty of testimonials to the value of having someone outside the organisation to act as sounding-board, advisor and occasionally guide. As far as I know, however, the claim has not been made that mentoring or coaching of this nature develops leadership at any level. I go to the doctor when I need some advice or help, but he is not giving me any teaching.

The line manager – alias the team, operational or strategic leader – is in a strong position to teach: the opportunity is there. He or she should do it not just by example – always the best teacher in this field – but also by talking. Some use Socratic conversations, where the art and practice of good leadership is explored together in a shared quest.

> **"**I learned most not from those who taught me, but from those who talked with me.**"**
>
> St Augustine

CHECKLIST

LINE MANAGERS AS LEADERSHIP MENTORS

	YES	NO
As a result of leadership training, do all managers and other leaders in your organisation spend time with each individual in their team?	☐	☐
Apart from semi-formal target-setting (or agreeing) and progress reviews, do these meetings touch upon personal and professional development?	☐	☐
Is appraisal seen as essentially a developmental means and not as an adjunct to the annual salary review?	☐	☐
Do you know the name of the leader in your organisation who is the star developer of people?	☐	☐
Have you offered line managers any training opportunities in how to become more effective mentors or coaches?	☐	☐
Do line managers always meet individual colleagues in their teams before and after they go on any internal or external developmental programme?	☐	☐

In what three ways has your own immediate superior helped you to become a better leader/team member as a result of your conversations on a one-to-one basis:

1..

2..

3..

KEY POINTS

- Most successful leaders can look back upon one or two persons who acted as leadership mentors in their careers. Such mentors are natural teachers. Being wise – intelligent, experienced and good – they can also act as counsellors or guides pointing out a path forwards in times of perplexity.

- All line managers are potential mentors. They can become active mentors by taking a personal interest in those who work for them. That means finding time to listen, to offer encouragement, to delegate, to coach if necessary, and to give some guidance if asked. If you do the spadework of mentoring in this way the chemistry of the relationship will usually look after itself.

- Some managers are uninspired leaders because no one has ever taken the time to inspire them. Inspiration is contagious; leadership is caught as well as taught.

- The best mentors are the least conspicuous.

- Anyone who expects to join a top team should be able to prove that he or she has developed at least three people capable of doing his or her existing job.

- Wisdom is not the prerogative of the old – there is no fool like an old fool. A good mentor has natural teaching ability, which draws the best from you. If you have found a good mentor, then thank God – or Athena – for him or her.

- Leadership is best learnt by being apprenticed to a leader, and the sign of a good master is delight when the pupil excels his own standard. Only the secure are humble.

"We learn only from those we love."
Johann Wolfgang Von Goethe

9 ▪ SELF-DEVELOPMENT

"Development is always self-development. Nothing could be more absurd than for an enterprise to assume responsibility for the development of a person."

Peter Drucker

"The ancient Japanese art of Bonsai uses subtle wiles and infinite pains to restrict the growth of a potentially mighty tree. Yet the same effect can be achieved in your career in management by quite the opposite process. By doing little or nothing. Which is why it is so important to take action. And to do it before the rot sets in."

So began an imaginative advertisement for a management course. Can people develop their own capabilities or possibilities themselves? Clearly the answer is yes: they can. In any sphere we can contribute a great deal to the process of professional or personal growth. That principle applies to leadership. As Field-Marshal Lord Slim said, 'There is nobody who cannot vastly improve his powers of leadership by a little thought and practice.'

BUILDING A CORPORATE CULTURE THAT ENCOURAGES LEADERSHIP LEARNING

In order to grow anything the climate has to be right. Leadership develops in a climate or atmosphere of trust, while it withers in a climate of distrust, suspicion, and cynicism.

It is in the night sky of corporate values – the stars by which the organisation steers its course – that we should look for the twin values of leadership and learning. Of course learning – the constant process of self-development – will encompass much more beside leadership. Both are contagious. If team leaders see that their operational and strategic leaders are humble enough to be open to learn more, then wild horses will not keep them from learning. Such is the power of example. As Edmund Burke said, 'Example is the school of mankind, and they will learn at no other.'

TEACHING OR LEARNING?

'I am always ready to learn but I do not always like being taught,' Winston Churchill once remarked to a friend.

To learn

To gain knowledge or understanding of or skill in by thought, study, instruction or experience.

To teach

Applies to any manner of imparting knowledge, information or skill so that others may learn. 'Teach' usually suggests a guided process of assigned work, discipline, directed study, and the presentation of examples. It may or may not indicate an academic context.

You can see that learning and teaching are actually complementary activities – or they should be. Much depends on the manner in which we are taught. Few of us like to be compulsorily on the receiving end of one-way transmission of information about a subject we are not interested in – alas, too often the fate of our children at school. As St Augustine observed, one learns more from teaching that resembles conversation – a dialogue not monologue – than from the formal lecture.

Yet learning without a teacher does not get very far. We call it learning by experience, but graduation from the university of experience takes a long time and the fees are high. What good teachers – teachers with knowledge and skill – do is to cut down the time spent learning from experience. They introduce ideas that are like catalysts in the learning process. The functional leadership course outlined on p64 is an example of a programme designed with the learning process as its foundation:

It is essential here to bear in mind that we learn in the more specific sense of that word by the interaction of principles or theory and experience or practice. It is when sparks jump between these two poles – the general and the actual – that learning occurs. So you need both. The various practical exercises, case-studies and examples in the training course are designed to be stepping-stones: see Figure 9.1.

Figure 9.1 The interaction between theory and practice

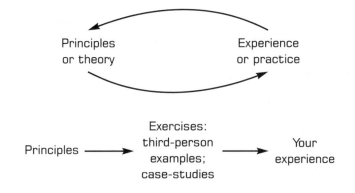

Equally the process must work in reverse. Your practical knowledge, gleaned from both observation of actual leaders and your own practical experience, must be brought to bear in a constructively critical way on the ideas presented in the course – or on this book for that matter.

'Learn' comes from a Latin word meaning a furrow or track. Like 'lead', it is a journey word. A teacher is a leader or guide to someone who is turning over new ground or walking down an unfamiliar track. Teacher and learner are walking side-by-side, partners in the enterprise of learning, for the best teachers are always the best learners. As Chaucer wrote of his Oxford scholar, 'Gladly would he learn and gladly teach.'

THE STRATEGIC IMPORTANCE OF BOOKS ON LEADERSHIP

My father, in effect an orphan, had to leave school at 14 years old to find work and support his grandparents. Eventually he became a field sales manager. In those distant 1930s there were no business schools, management courses or in-company programmes, certainly not on leadership. To pay for his children's education he bought second-hand books on his sales travels and sold them to Foyles in London. He taught himself and his salesmen leadership by reading business books. Ordway Tead's *The art of leadership* (1935), which I have mentioned already, was fortunately on his shelves and I learnt a lot from it while I was still at school.

Books are simply teachers talking to you on paper. To those disposed to learn they are still the most efficient means of acquiring what above I called principles or theory.

Books were in fact the first great learning revolution: they put knowledge literally in the hands of the learner. Xenophon, the father of leadership studies, wrote books on leadership that were read by – among others – Alexander the Great, Scipio Africanus (the conqueror of Hannibal), Cicero and Julius Caesar. In the Dark Ages we lost both the books on leadership and the tradition of learning leadership directly from great teachers through the written word. Those who want to learn to lead always say they benefit from reading books on leadership or about leaders. They may not teach you anything new, but they confirm what you know, refresh and stimulate you and sometimes – in a quiet moment – rekindle the fires of enthusiasm in you. Every book, even the dullest ones, usually have one bright pearl in them for you, if you search for it.

Once that flame is lit, once a leader finds his or her feet on that inward and invisible path of leadership, then the whole world becomes a book. We learn by experience and reflection; we learn by apprenticeship and observation; we learn from other leaders and by glimpsing the greatness of spirit in those who face and endure adversity. As we say in English, all is grist to the mill – that is, all is useful or profitable to an aspiring leader, especially when added to what already exists. (Grist, for those unfamiliar with the word, is that quantity of grain that is to be ground at any one time.) And from the grist we make our daily bread – the leadership that we are able to offer as a gift to others.

> **"**Learning which does not advance each day will daily decrease.**"**
>
> Chinese proverb

CHECKLIST

SELF-DEVELOPMENT

	YES	NO
Would you describe yourself personally as being on a track of learning – a path of exploring and learning about leadership?	☐	☐
Has anyone ever mentioned curiosity as one of your qualities?	☐	☐
Can you list the names of three people who have been your principal teachers of leadership:	☐	☐

1...

2...

3...

	YES	NO
Do you believe that the culture of your organisation is one that grows leadership?	☐	☐
Among the stars by which your organisation navigates would an external observer identify leadership and learning as two cardinal values?	☐	☐

List the five values that characterise your culture now, and the five that you would like to see there in 2010:

NOW   2010

1.. 1..

2.. 2..

3.. 3..

4.. 4..

5.. 5..

◼ KEY POINTS

- Self-help is essential. Organisations should encourage all their employees – not just the managers or leaders – to develop themselves as leaders and team members.

- Training courses in leadership are no more than opportunities for those who wish to learn. You cannot teach people leadership – you can only help them to find it within themselves.

- In order to develop oneself, theory or principles must be brought to bear upon one's practice or experience. Books and other distance learning methods have a part to play in that process.

- You cannot ride a bicycle until someone gives you a bicycle. Self-development is best done by doing the work of a leader, not thinking or reading about it. Action first, then reflection.

- Mentors – experienced leaders – can be an immense help to the young manager. Self-development includes seeking out these teachers and benefiting from what they have to say.

- Learning is a gradual process of absorbing, testing and re-testing; you try something – it works in some circumstances, not others – you reflect.

- Leaders are seasoned by failure. Failure teaches success. If you are not making mistakes you are not trying hard enough.

"The lyf so short, the craft so long to lerne."
Chaucer *Parliament of Foules* 1386

10 ■ THE STRATEGIC LEADER

"As the chief man of the city is, so will the people be."

Ecclesiastes

There are two errors to avoid in thinking about the strategic leader or director-in-chief of an organisation. The first error is to exaggerate the importance of that one person. Some people believe that if only they can find a hero in shining armour, a 'knight on a white horse', to lead them, salvation will follow as surely as day follows night. In political life the world has seen this doctrine carried to its extremes, in the last century in the horrors of fascism: *Der Führer* and *Il Duce* were the German and Italian words for 'the Leader'.

The other error is to go to the opposite end of the pole and dispense with a single leader at the top altogether. This usually means rule by a committee or an oligarchy of some kind. That solution can work quite well if things are running smoothly. But change, especially in the form of crisis, throws up the need for swift decisions and leadership from one person.

The truth lies between these extremes. All does not depend on the strategic leader. The quality of the senior group of leaders – the strategic leadership team – around him or her, the degree of leadership exercised throughout the organisation, not to mention a host of contingent factors like materiel and luck, will help to determine the eventual outcome. Hannibal and the elephants of Carthage could not overcome Rome, nor could Robert E. Lee and his Confederates vanquish the Northern States, though both Hannibal and Lee were the finest leaders of their day. The most inspirational head teacher will struggle to turn around a failing school if the teachers are not competent and properly trained and the parents supportive.

Equally, an organisation that lacks good leadership at the top carries a heavy handicap in the competitive race. Yet it may have the staying power to survive until it finds the right leadership. Rome's great strength and resources gave it time to find a leader in Scipio Africanus who could eventually beat Carthage. The Northern States of America, under the inspiring leadership of Abraham Lincoln, also had time on their side – after much trial and error Lincoln eventually found his general in Ulysses S. Grant. The dedication of a hospital's medical staff or the quality of a business's product may enable them to get by with inadequate leadership, but the appointment of an exceptional chief executive will be required to take performance to a higher level.

To summarise: large organisations and institutions, like nations, are led by a team of leaders – at team, operational and strategic levels. But that leadership team itself needs a leader, a *primus inter pares* or first among equals, just as an orchestra needs a conductor.

THE RISE OF THE CHIEF EXECUTIVE

In times of crisis, as history shows many times, free and democratic peoples tend to entrust power to one person to see them through. The exercise of that power is usually limited in extent by law, and limited in duration. When the crisis was over, republics such as Rome expected their dictators to emulate the worthy Cincinnatus, who resigned his dictatorship after the 16 days during which he had vanquished the foe, then returned to his farm beyond the Tiber.

Economic recession produces much the same tendency in industry and commerce to strengthen the positional power of the person at the top, so as to free him or her to make the necessary decisions, to cut out the dead wood and to provide firm, tough but fair leadership in the right direction. The title 'chief executive' which came into vogue about two decades ago, reflected the shift of emphasis.

'Executive' is, of course, the standard American word for 'manager'. It makes explicit the essential nature of a manager (as opposed to a leader or director), as one who carries out or executes policies or directives of others. Significantly an executive officer in the armed forces of the United States is the officer who is always second in-command. The executive branch of government in the United States is the branch responsible for carrying out the policies agreed by Senate and Congress. In business language, then, an executive is any person who holds a position of administrative or managerial responsibility.

In Britain it became common for a board of directors to appoint a general manager to supervise the work of other managers running the business. In the course of time the powers of the general manager were extended beyond supervision. As some senior managers became executive directors on the board, the general manager changed his or her title to 'managing director'.

A director-general of the British Institute of Directors, Jan Hildreth, was among the first to note the growing use of the chief executive title:

> **"**If there is a distinction between the role of the managing director and the chief executive – and I believe there is – it is one of the degree of leadership required from each.
>
> The managing director must run the show from his or her position as an equal among his fellow board members. The chief executive must lead both the board and the organisation; this includes running the people who are running the show.
>
> In essence, the chief executive represents a fine compromise between the need of any human organisation for a recognisable leader, and the needs of the parties interested in an enterprise for a committee to protect and balance their interests.
>
> To succeed, or even to survive, in this most difficult of roles requires of the chief executive good health, humour, a resilience not given to many, and the powers of persuasion and personal leadership needed in both boardroom and workshop.**"**

Incidentally, the title of director-general was another import into Britain during the 1970s. It is the French equivalent to chief executive.

THE CHIEF EXECUTIVE'S CONTRIBUTION TO LEADERSHIP DEVELOPMENT

In *Effective strategic leadership* (Adair 2002) I propose that the generic role of strategic leader in terms of the three-circles model breaks down naturally into seven generic functions. The relevant one in this context is *selecting and developing leaders for today and tomorrow.* Therefore, as I mentioned above, the strategic leader is really the person to whom this book should be addressed – I hope you will give him or her a copy! If the chief executive picks up the torch, then you are in business. If not – I can only say personally that trying to develop leadership in an organisation where the chief executive is indifferent, disengaged or hostile is about as close as I have ever got to wasting my time. Never again.

These days, fortunately, that attitude of 'It's good for junior managers but not for me,' or 'Leadership? You must talk to personnel or training about that' is a thing of the past. An effective strategic leader will be leading by example in the field of leadership development, what all leaders in the organisation should do and be. He or she should be able to talk about the values of the organisation, which will include good leadership at all levels.

James Callaghan, a former British prime minister, once told me that he had only ever read one book on leadership (alas, not one of mine), but had he done so before he became prime minister he thought he would have made a better job of it. This was an honest admission, subsequently repeated in a published lecture in the United States. As our culture slowly changes, senior leaders at all levels – including the national and global political level – will come to see that they are on the inner learning journey.

YOUR RESPONSIBILITY FOR THE CORPORATE CULTURE

The corporate culture or ethos of an organisation – its core values and underlying philosophy – are important indeed vital for several reasons. In this context I simply want to make the point that some cultures – like ICI in the 1980s – grow leaders and some stunt leadership. And it is the strategic leader's responsibility to ensure that there is a strong and positive culture.

Culture, ethos and climate are words that point to an intangible but highly important dimension of leadership development. 'Culture' means the way of living, thinking and feeling of a group of people following a common set of values. A key ingredient in cultures that grow leaders is the value they place on learning, reflected in the giving of encouragement, opportunity and example.

A common knowledge or tradition about leaders and what they do is a core ingredient in organisational cultures in which leaders grow. Such organisations have one characteristic in common: they place a high value on leadership in command or management and insist on its presence.

Example is contagious, be it good or bad. An organisation with a high proportion of good leaders – and leaders for good – will develop a climate conducive to nurturing leadership.

Other important elements in organisational climate include a proper delegation of authority. It stems from a warmth of relations and a mutual trust between levels of leadership, based in turn on mutual perception of professional competence and personal integrity.

'Morale' describes a group or organisation's attitude to its work. Strategic leaders are there to create a high morale and a positive atmosphere in organisations, so that they can successfully achieve their tasks. It is in that kind of atmosphere that creativity and innovation flourish.

Changing an organisation's culture when necessary is one of the supreme challenges for a strategic leader. Is it one that you face now? Alternatively, you may feel relatively happy with the corporate culture of your organisation at present. But remember that can change, either suddenly or insidiously, for the worse, and if it does so then you are the one who is accountable.

When it comes to the values and ethos of the organisation, which one day you should hand on to another's care in better shape than when you found it, you have only two watchwords: *eternal vigilance.*

A PERSONAL WORD TO YOUR CHIEF EXECUTIVE

Nobody expects top leaders to be perfect in terms of personal qualities, professional knowledge – so they never make mistakes – or performance of key leadership functions. In fact great leaders are often great in both their strengths and their faults. It follows that lesser leaders also have their contradictions.

Groups or organisations allow for the realities of human nature and they give an 'idiosyncrasy credit' to their leaders. Providing you score enough marks in the task, team and individual circles your human frailties will be tolerated. Good team members will complement your skills and cover up your deficiencies. Perfection is not part of the job description, but people will respond well if they sense that you are leading to the best of your ability.

Visits to courses for developing leadership and teamwork within the organisation ought to come high on the list of priorities for a chief executive. Apart from providing an opportunity to underline the message of the course and its relevance to the organisation in a rapidly changing world, such occasions allow the chief executive to talk about the strategic thrust of the business and listen to the reactions of a cross-section of managers or employers. Taking people into your counsel – showing them the cards – is a powerful way of motivating them. Your presence confers recognition both on the subject and on the actual or potential contributions of those present.

> **"**Example is not the main thing in influencing others – it is the only thing.**"**
> Albert Schweitzer

CHECKLIST

THE STRATEGIC LEADER

To be completed by your chief executive.

	YES	NO
Do you accept that you do 'own' the problem of developing leaders at all levels of the organisation?	☐	☐
Are you satisfied with the existing strategy for leadership development?	☐	☐
Have you matched your vision and sense of purpose for the organisation with a set of core values?	☐	☐

With that statement of values in front of you, please tick if the following words occur:

☐ integrity ☐ leadership ☐ social responsibility

☐ honesty ☐ fairness or justice ☐ learning

Have you taken steps to improve your ability as a public speaker?	☐	☐
Is there a mentor with whom you can discuss issues, problems or opportunities facing you as a leader?	☐	☐

Write down the last biography of a leader or book about leadership that you read:

....

Choose one strategic leader you admire. What are the three lessons you learnt from him/her?

1...

2...

3...

When did you last work for a week on the shop floor or its equivalent?

KEY POINTS

- Organisational effectiveness benefits greatly from good leadership at the top, but it is not wholly dependent upon it.

- Greater power and influence are accorded to chief executives or their equivalents, but there are also greater expectations of leadership focused on them.

- Leaders of very large organisations do well when they set the broad strategy, create the right climate and develop the business leaders needed for today – and tomorrow.

- Chief executives can influence positively the growth of leadership at all levels by their words, their example and their presence in the training context.

- If the chief executive does not take action to develop leadership at boardroom level – and one step below – no one else will.

And more advice

Nowadays it is a requirement of a strategic leader that you should be able to talk about leadership within the organisation. Talk about the business first, how it is doing and where it is going.

Then say directly what you expect from leaders. Be clear, simple, concise and vivid. Salt with humour; add the spice of challenge.

If you have the humility to learn in order to move from being a good strategic leader, you will create a culture of self-development throughout the organisation.

> "To act is easy; to think is hard."
> Johann Wolfgang Von Goethe

3 PRINCIPLES IN ACTION

▪ INTRODUCTION

The seven case studies in this part are illustrations of the range, versatility and depth of practical philosophy of leadership development outlined in this book. They speak for themselves, but you may like to bear in mind some key questions as you read them and then, so to speak, put your questions to the contributors and see how far their case studies contain clear indications as to how they would answer them.

The first and most important set of questions is: Why are you doing it? Why do you perceive leadership development to be important?

Then ask yourself: Why did the contributors choose the ACL approach? Can you see any common pattern in the training values they see in my model and its associated philosophy? What keeps them using it year-on-year?

That takes us on to the really key question: Does it work? Is the training effective in producing 'not bosses but leaders'? Is it due to the success factor that they stick with it? How cost-effective is ACL? Can it live up to its promise of being high volume, high quality and low cost?

Last, keep your eye on the trainers. It is essential to design programmes that, like aircraft, will take off, fly and perform beautifully with an experienced pilot at the controls. But it is impossible to eliminate completely the possibility of pilot error. The organisations and individuals represented in these case studies set high standards for themselves in delivering ACL – but they get great results. How do they 'train the trainers'?

I am not pretending that any organisation using my philosophy as a foundation for its leadership developments, or any individual trainer skilled in ACL, is perfect. There is always room for improvement; perfection eludes us – but excellence is within your grasp. These case studies will give you a good idea of what is possible in this field, and point the way to excellence.

CASE STUDY 1

ACTION-CENTRED LEADERSHIP IN THE SCOTTISH POLICE

Although it is hard to determine an exact date, it is thought that ACL has been provided as part of management and leadership training at the Scottish Police College at Tulliallan Castle since the 1970s. At that time the police service was an organisation that operated on a largely command and control basis, and therefore the action-centred approach was a highly appropriate model for the service. It was a model that police officers could easily relate to, largely due to its historical development as a leadership tool for military officers. It would be fair to say that the vast majority of police supervisors in Scotland today have received training on ACL. Indeed it is a model that has withstood the test of time because to this day, first-line managers, including police officers and support staff (civilian supervisors), still receive an input on the action-centred approach within the Leadership and Management Division (the division that provides core leadership training for police officers and civilian support staff) of the college.

When ACL was first introduced to the Scottish Police College it was provided to all leaders as a package that took two and a half days to deliver. The sergeants initially received limited training; however, this gradually developed into the full package. For many supervisory officers ACL provided their first exposure to a model that would allow them to take a more scientific approach towards leading their teams. The ACL model provided most people with a point of reference to measure their performance as a leader against. In many instances the ACL model provided positive reinforcement, or additional guidance, for leaders who had used their common sense and experience to survive as newly promoted officers, prior to attending the appropriate course at the Scottish Police College.

The training was initially provided by a team of six chief inspectors who were seconded as instructors to the then Senior Division (now Leadership and Management Division) of the college. The tutors were initially trained by The Industrial Society which accredited staff members to its standard. The tutors were trained to a high standard and well motivated to develop the future leaders of the Scottish Police Service.

The training proved to be popular with students, who enjoyed the blend of theory and practical exercises to reinforce the learning. All of the students who experienced ACL training soon became familiar with practical exercises which involved tasks including building jigsaws, sorting cards and building Lego bridges and cars. The tasks were equally shared among the students, and for each exercise one student was selected to be the leader. The leader was provided with a briefing by the tutor, a team of four students and a box full of resources to complete the task. These exercises were carried out against the clock within a syndicate room, and on completion of the exercise a full debrief was carried out by the tutors.

Students also gained valuable learning points by comparing and contrasting two different leadership styles as portrayed in the film *Twelve O'Clock High* (1949). The opportunity to view a black and white vintage movie starring Gregory Peck, Gary Merrill and Dean Jagger also provided a welcome break from the more intensive training, particularly the practical exercises. Many students did question the use of such an old film for training purposes. However when the tutor took time to explain the underpinning logic and sensitivity of the film, most students gained a great deal of learning.

The case study was broken into two main parts. The first looked at the leadership of Colonel Davenport, played by Gary Merrill, who was very popular with his troops, but was suffering from stress and not achieving the task. The second part focused on the leadership of Brigadier General Frank Savage, played by Gregory Peck, who took over from Davenport and through a series of actions managed to make the 918th Bomb Group a more effective and motivated team. The case study was used to effectively reinforce much of the theory with practical examples of the types of actions that a successful leader requires to take to be effective.

During the 1970s and 1980s most senior officers in the Scottish Police Service completed ACL training. As many of these officers progressed through the ranks, the Scottish Police College had to take action to prevent the occurrence of repeated training. To avoid this danger the ACL package began to be delivered exclusively to sergeants and inspectors. Both of these ranks received the full two and a half days package, and after a number of years the inspectors' training was reduced to one day only.

As the decades passed by the ACL package remained very popular with students who consistently evaluated highly the training provided by staff in the Senior Division. The relevance and effectiveness of the ACL training was reviewed on a regular basis, particularly when new leadership models emerged from the academic world. However due to the excellent feedback from students and the pragmatic nature of the ACL package, the training survived various reviews.

While ACL was mainly provided to police supervisors as a leadership tool, it was also used for other purposes. Several divisions at Tulliallan used ACL tasks as part of their assessment procedures to measure the potential and ability of applicants for posts at the college. This use of ACL continued for many years until changes in the application and interviewing procedures for potential staff members were aligned to comply with equal opportunities legislation.

As already stated, ACL is still delivered in Leadership and Management Division to this day. The training is now part of a two-day module on leadership which was developed by Inspector Kenny Degnan and Miss Wendy Jones. Sergeants and support staff supervisors are provided with training in ACL on the first day of their course. This is a deliberate strategy in that the exercises very quickly help syndicate members to bond and get to know each other. On the second day of the module the students are provided with an input on an adapted version of Hersey and Blanchard's model on the situational approach to leadership. Both models together provide a powerful set of tools for first-line managers.

ACL is also provided as a part of inputs for other college courses. For example the leadership input for the Intelligence Manager's Course re-examines ACL in light of the role of supervisor within the intelligence community. Most leaders in these posts agree that ACL still has a role to play in this fairly hi-tech area of modern policing. The intelligence manager's role focused firmly on achieving tasks within tight time constraints. However, the intelligence community acknowledge that failure to develop their individuals and build teams will reduce their ability to perform effectively. This is indeed the essence of the action-centred approach.

William Allan
Chief Inspector
Programme Co-ordinator
Leadership and Management Division
Scottish Police College

Note

There have been several name changes in the Scottish Police College Division that provides ACL training:

1970–1999	Senior Division
1999–2004	Management Development Division
2004–Present	Leadership and Management Division

CASE STUDY 2

RAF USE OF ACTION-CENTRED LEADERSHIP

The British military have always considered leadership crucial – it has been a major subject at its officer schools since they were set up – and Professor John Adair's functional approach to leadership found a ready and fertile audience in the Royal Air Force as the first practical leadership theory promoting good teamwork.

The Royal Air Force College Cranwell, and its sister organisation the Officer Cadet Training Unit at Henlow, were training young officers in just 24 weeks by the time John Adair's approach to leadership was adopted. Both schools, therefore, wholeheartedly adopted the functional approach to leadership with its easy to remember and practical focus represented by the three interlocking circles: task, team and individual. The two practical leadership camps that all officer cadets undertook as part of their training at that time (and still do) were totally focused on the Adair model, and proved time and again the utility of the theory. Throughout the subsequent years of training young officers for the Royal Air Force, both the College at Cranwell and the Officer Cadet Training Unit at Henlow have used the functional approach to leadership espoused by Professor John Adair.

Today, the Royal Air Force is much smaller and more efficient, and there is a 'single-gate' entry into the officer corps through the Royal Air Force College. Young officers are trained in 26 weeks before continuing to their specialist training. Since John Adair first formed his functional approach to leadership theory, a plethora of people have written and pontificated on the subject of leadership. In fact were you to acquire all the books on leadership listed by Amazon.com and read one every day, it would take you 39 years to read them all (Grint 2004) – yet still the three circles have a central position in the teaching of leadership at the College.

"There are many ways of defining leadership and the essential qualities and behaviour of a leader. [The Officer and Aircrew Cadet Training Unit] uses 6 major approaches in an attempt to give a balanced perspective on leadership thinking. These are the Qualities, Situational, Contingency, Transactional and Transformational brought into practical focus by Adair's Action-Centred Leadership."

Notes to Cadets, Section 8: Leadership (2003)

Adair's action-centred approach is the most practical that is currently taught at the Royal Air Force College; it is the building block that the Royal Air Force uses for all approaches. The following extract from the current *Notes to Cadets* Section 8: Leadership sets out the current teaching of ACL. It shows how enduring the theory has been:

The 3 areas of need are now further broken down into actions taken, to achieve the task, to maintain the team's cohesion and to satisfy the individual needs of the team member.

TASK: Defining the Task
Making a Plan
Allocating Work & Resources
Controlling Quality & Tempo of Work
Checking Performance against the Plan
Adjusting the Plan

TEAM: Setting Standards
Maintaining Discipline
Building Team Spirit
Encouraging, Motivating, giving a sense of purpose
Appointing sub-leaders
Ensuring Communication within the group
Training the Group
Ensuring Welfare of the Team

INDIVIDUAL: Attending to personal problems
Encouraging individuals
Giving status
Recognizing and using individual attributes
Training the Individual
Ensuring Welfare of the Individual

Figure 11.1 The three-circles model

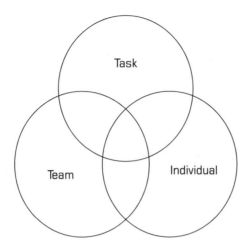

These 3 areas can visualized as 3 circles, all overlapping, remove one circle and gaps are created, the actions of a leader in one area can directly affect one or both of the other areas, for example motivating the team and encouraging the individual. The art is to understand when and how, to apply priorities. No one area of need is always dominant. Priorities will change by the situation that the team finds itself in. The common perception is that the military leader is task-orientated to the detriment of the team and team members. An effective leader is one who assesses each situation on its merits and adopts a suitable approach to match.

Beyond simple task-orientated leadership, there are three levels of leadership that officers will encounter during their RAF career:

a. Tactical – Close-in team focused.
b. Operational – Culture, management style and energy.
c. Strategic – Vision, direction and the future.

None of these layers are mutually exclusive or rank driven; as a junior officer your staff will look to you to provide their direction and to clearly articulate the corporate vision. We have considered leadership theories and approaches and established the need for a focus or leader when working in teams. We must now consider how we put into practice these theories.

The 26-week Initial Officer Training Course currently being used at the Royal Air Force College is under review as I write, and a new course will be introduced next year. This slightly longer course will have leadership as its single most important and largest element. It will be teaching yet more theories and practices of leadership, yet Professor John Adair's action-centred leadership will still provide the new cadets with its eminently practical tool that has stood the test of time. After all, Reece and Walker (1992) say, 'learning is more effective if it is based on experiences .... Concepts that are able to be practised or seen are more likely to be learned better.'

Leadership training for the non-commissioned officers of the Royal Air Force has developed in a different way. Most leadership training for non-commissioned officers is done within the Airman's Command Squadron. Since the 1980s, training courses for NCOs began to use the functional approach to leadership introduced by Professor John Adair. The courses metamorphosed over time into the current Management, Leadership and Command courses run by the Airman's Command Squadron. They too have endured with the three circles of task, team and individual so familiar to all who have been introduced to the functional approach to leadership.

The Airman's Command Squadron run three courses on Management, Leadership and Command, for those on promotion to corporal, sergeant and flight sergeant respectively. They also have introduced the study of many of the new and emerging theories on leadership to these courses: Hersey/Blanchard's situational leadership, the transformational approach (Hooper and Potter 1997), transformational and transactional leadership (Stephen Covey 1992), Emotional intelligence (Daniel Goleman 1998) and mission command to name a few. However, only the flight sergeants are taught the issues of strategic and operational leadership. Transformational and transactional theory is only taught to sergeants and flight sergeants, and so with all the others. The only one of all those theories taught on all three courses that the Squadron runs is Professor John Adair's functional approach to leadership.

In 2003 the senior commanders of the Royal Air Force set up the Royal Air Force Leadership Centre with the remit to provide coherent, through-life leadership training to all RAF personnel. After one year of operation, the Leadership Centre has provided strategic guidance and doctrine for leadership within the Royal Air Force. Within our approach, Professor John Adair's functional approach to leadership will remain as part of the leadership teaching to all commissioned and non-commissioned officers in the Royal Air Force. It will provide them with one of the tools with which they can develop excellence in their leadership as their predecessors have done before them.

Group Captain John Jupp
Head Royal Air Force Leadership Centre

CASE STUDY 3

ACTION-CENTRED LEADERSHIP IN ARMENIA

Armenia is a landlocked republic with Turkey to the west, Georgia to the north, Azerbaijan to the east, and Iran to the south. It is a Christian country surrounded by Muslim states. Once known as the Soviet 'Silicon Valley', the economy faltered when its traditional USSR markets disappeared. Although the economy has partly recovered, poverty reduction and job creation have not kept pace with current growth, and the country also suffers from a trade embargo with its neighbours as a result of land disputes. Over 50 per cent of the population is below the poverty line, and on top of all this officialdom, along with leadership of commerce and industry, is plagued by corrupt practice. Ethical leadership is a rare gem found in only a few places (and hearts).

At the leading edge of the move to change things are two young men of outstanding moral integrity who founded the Centre for Leadership Development (CLD) four years ago in the capital, Yerevan. Their mission statement is worth considering:

> **"**To equip and develop a new generation of leaders of integrity and excellence who will transform Armenian society for the lasting good.**"**

CLD students are carefully selected through a rigorous selection procedure that looks for the four 'Cs' of calling, character, competence and community spirit. Places are vied for and only 40 each semester are chosen from more than 200 applicants. The CLD sets a high bar.

Alan Gogbashian and Stepan Avanessian are the co-founders of CLD, and they wage a constant battle for survival on two key fronts: funding through sponsorship, and the finding of quality teachers of integrity and humility who can lead CLD students towards personal growth; and do it *pro bono publico.*

Barry Chester, regional general manager of human resources for Mitsubishi Corporation in Europe, the Middle East and Africa, was invited to train CLD students in the fall semester of 2004. The stated instruction from the founders was to provide very practical managerial and leadership training to balance the more academic lectures planned for the rest of the semester. They also requested that any models or theories used had to be practical and easily understood. At this point it is useful to note that only about one-third of the students had a good command of English, so all sessions would require handouts and other materials translated into Armenian, and a simultaneous translation of all that was to be said in class.

Chester's response was to design a learning event in two parts; a delivery of a practical model of leadership, the John Adair action-centred leadership (ACL) circles in the first session, and the practical implementation of the ACL model during a whole-day leadership and teamwork simulation. Chester selected the ACL because it was simple to use and explain, and had stood the test of time. The circle diagrams are practical and provide a clear and strong leadership message, particularly in the overlapping areas of the circles. This translates into any language. The three circles also have a very functional and situational dimension which is again easy to understand and teach.

The first session took place on a Thursday evening (as most students either worked or were at university during the day). Chester began by explaining the history of leadership theory in three parts:

- the qualities approach (emphasising what you are)

- the situational approach (emphasising what you know)

- the functional approach (emphasising what you do).

The functional approach being the basis of ACL, Chester stressed the practical application of leadership through dealing with the task, the team, and the individual. He rounded the initial period off by discussing a few satellite theories that reinforce the vitality of ACL. These were Herzberg's two-factor theory, Maslow's hierarchy of needs, and the Tannenbaum and Schmidt continuum [these are all explained elsewhere in this book]. He closed the period by discussing the principles of motivation and the role of the leader. Some brief group work was involved to flush out key points.

The second period of the evening session was devoted to leadership planning, a critical component of success in any leadership endeavour. This session was concluded by an explanation of Bruce Truckman's team development stages (forming, storming, norming, reforming and adjourning). Chester warned the students to expect to proceed through these stages during the simulation exercise, and to plan to deal with each stage as the leader (or a leader) recognised it. In this manner, the students were prepared for the rigours of Saturday.

Chester had carefully considered how best to display the leadership elements of task, team and individual so that students could believe in and therefore internalise the learning provided. He designed a simulation based on a real event in Armenia, an earthquake. The area around Gyumri in the north of the country was devastated by an earthquake in 1988, and tens of thousands lost their lives. The simulation touched many components of the kind of leadership that CLD required: humanity, compassion, competence, and strength of heart to succeed against all barriers. It also needed a sense of mission, skilled analysis, careful planning and assessed risk management.

The simulation placed the team in a situation where they had to respond to the emergency and receive, safeguard and transport essential supplies across the ravaged country to an isolated community destroyed by a major seismic event and desperate for food, blankets and aid. There was a tight time constraint and a lack of resources. Rail and road systems were down and information was scarce. Many problems were written into the simulation to prevent or delay delivery using a choice of several routes, only one of which was completely safe.

Several teams of five or six students were formed and the exercise was constructed as a competition to see which team delivered the most aid by the deadline. The teams selected their own leaders, and each team had access to exactly the same (limited) information as all other teams. Each team had a trained observer whose job was to watch and record every significant action the leader and the team did. Their role was to provide detailed end-of-simulation feedback. They used an observation checklist based on the ACL functions in order to be able to provide clear statements of strong and 'not so strong' actions observed during the day. Chester also roved about during the day taking notes of events so he could deliver a big-picture plenary session at the end.

The exercise took five hours and was immediately followed by a one-hour feedback and self-evaluation session with the observers. Chester then provided his personal view of events, giving emphasis to his observations of leader actions and any resulting team or individual reactions. The ACL model proved extremely useful because it provided a common language using task, team and individual elements, as well as the key functional definitions. This all helped to bridge the simultaneous translation issues.

Personal action plans were written by all students, and these were also based on the ACL framework. Each student considered his or her own responses to the exercise and the feedback from the various observers and team colleagues. Each individual now has a precise idea of what went well, what was a problem, and what he or she needs to do to translate the learning into a personal leadership plan for growth.

The CLD in Armenia has been overwhelmed with positive student responses to the ACL model used in conjunction with a practical team and leadership exercise. The three circles have easily transcended culture and language. It has left a lasting impression on many young servant leaders of tomorrow, in what we all hope will be a more ethical Armenia as a result of their contribution to change for good.

CASE STUDY 4

■ ROYAL NAVY LEADERSHIP TRAINING AND ACTION-CENTRED LEADERSHIP: LEADERSHIP TRAINING OF YOUNG OFFICERS AT BRITANNIA ROYAL NAVAL COLLEGE (BRNC)

Britannia Royal Naval College (BRNC) mostly trains officers who have just joined the Royal Navy. However the age of the trainees varies from 18 to in excess of 40. This wide range is a result of BRNC taking school leavers, university graduates and individuals who have been selected from the Ratings Corps for promotion to commissioned officer. The BRNC Leadership mission statement is:

"To ensure Cadets realise the leadership potential identified at the Admiral Interview Board."

The leadership modules are designed to get the trainees thinking about the qualities required of a leader and how to develop the characteristics to effectively lead a team. BRNC has moved away from the premise that leaders are born, and develops the idea that we all have innate leadership skills, but need to understand what these skills are in order to realise and develop them. Its staff also discuss how leadership is about getting things done, which is more than just achieving the job in hand; it has to do with training, preparation and organising for the future. Throughout these early stages the training staff at BRNC explain that one of the most fundamental levels of leadership comes down to an individual's own personality and character.

The theory that a group of people with a common aim or task has various needs that must be met if they are to be successful is further emphasised using the three areas of action-centred leadership (ACL), in that the leader must:

- achieve the task

- build and develop the team

- develop the individual.

Moving into the functional leadership arena, Adair's model of task, team and individual helps to demonstrate what appears to some to be an extremely complex subject, but is in fact quite straightforward and mainly common sense. The Adair three-circle model is used as a demonstration point, and the trainees are invited to think about how the importance of each circle alters depending upon the task in hand. This changing importance is illustrated by the use of examples of situations they might find themselves confronting in the future, such a fire on board a ship. With the fire example the task of extinguishing the fire and securing the safety of the ship becomes the obvious priority for the leader. However, when analysis for other routine day-to-day scenarios is conducted, the welfare of a person or the need to develop the team becomes the leader's main focus.

The BRNC staff also draw out from the trainees that the three circles have an influence on each other, and that they are interrelated. Within the Service the functional leadership model has proven to be understandable and easily used by individuals covering a wide variety of backgrounds. The model works and has been proven to work; whether in combat in the Operations Room of a ship under attack, on the bridge while transiting in convoy or during normal day-to-day routine tasks of maintaining the ship and the crew.

The functional leadership process that the model is provided with is known in BRNC as the 'big six'. This is a logical, common-sense sequence that can be applied to all situations, not just during the training. The big six are: aim, plan, brief, execute, evaluate and communicate.

Leadership and actions checklists are offered to the trainees. These checklists relate the big six leadership functions to Adair's three-circles model. These handouts have proved to be a useful and handy reminder of the steps involved with carrying out a task effectively.

Leadership training of non commissioned officers and ratings at HMS Collingswood

While the NCOs received some leadership development as part of their professional training from as early as 1741, specific leadership courses are a much more recent phenomenon, commencing in the 1940s at HMS Royal Arthur. The Royal Navy has always been a service with a wide and diverse range of people. However, it was the increase in management understanding in the 1950s and 1960s that led to a realisation that more than just basic leadership training was required. Since the early 1990s a more systematic approach has been used for the development of potential leaders. The three interactive circles of action-centred leadership (ACL) theory became the underlying bedrock, helping to forge a new beginning for the leaders in the Royal Navy within both the Officer and Rating Corps.

The Command Training Group Courses

The Command Training Group is responsible for conducting bespoke CLM training for all NCOs and Ratings within the service. This training is primarily delivered through a five-day outdoor teambuilding course to the newly joined Phase 2 trainees, some of whom have only 8 to 14 weeks' service in the Royal Navy. Two further levels of Command Courses are taught, varying in length from two to four weeks for more experienced personnel and as part of their preparation for promotion.

Phase 2 Outdoor Leadership Training Course

This five-day course is aimed at introducing and developing the teambuilding potential of the most junior personnel. The course provides instruction in the basic theoretical and practical aspects of teambuilding and leadership, and uses the medium of adventurous training to demonstrate teaching points. Trainees are given the opportunity to take charge of a small team conducting simple tasks under the supervision of the training staff.

By the end of this short introduction to leadership, each trainee will have demonstrated his or her ability to contribute to team performance, support the leader, contribute to defining the objectives and discussing the way forward prior to accepting the delegated task/s and achieving the aim. This course is the first opportunity that the service has to identify the potential future leaders of the Royal Navy.

Leading Ratings' Command Course

The aim of this course is to train personnel to be effective Leading Rates by developing their leadership qualities, instilling a sense of purpose, improving self-confidence, developing effective communication and understanding the responsibilities of becoming a Leading Rate and Superior Officer.

The following subjects are covered: ACL, motivation and morale, stress, communication, delegation, naval discipline and punishment, first aid, duties and responsibilities, problem-solving and brainstorming sessions, security and financial responsibility. Physical activities, which account for nearly 50 per cent of the course, include team obstacle course runs, a 25–30 mile trek across country using map and compass, daily physical exercise, swimming tests, parade training, and directed command tasks (utilising ACL). There are various discussion periods and problem-solving exercises. Additionally, all students deliver two lectures of their own choice in order to develop the art of good communication and enhance personal confidence when in front of others.

Students are continually assessed throughout training, with a comprehensive report outlining both performance and future potential. The report is compiled by the instructors and forwarded to a promotion board on completion of training.

Senior Ratings' Command Course

The primary aim of this course is to develop Senior Ratings (NCOs) to lead personnel in the Fleet. The following subjects are covered: ACL and situational leadership, including practical management, communication exercises, motivation and morale, stress management, naval discipline regulations, first aid, duties and responsibilities, security, decision-making and problem-solving scenarios, general naval knowledge, parade training and lecturing. Physical activities, which account for a significant part of the course, include team obstacle course runs, a 30–40 mile problem-solving trek across the Brecon Beacon range and bespoke directed command tasks. There are various periods devoted to management discussions and brainstorming sessions. Additionally, each student delivers a formal assessed lecture to help develop the art of communication and improve personal confidence.

Again students are continually assessed with a comprehensive report, outlining performance and future potential, compiled by the course instructors and forwarded to the promotion selection board on completion of course.

The command training rationale of 'getting things done'

In line with the principles of ACL, CTG has developed the "getting things done" model in order to give the Command Course students an understanding of how command interacts with leadership and management in order to achieve the task. This model is then used during practical scenarios.

- Command – the authority. Command gives the individual the authority to direct.

- Management – the ability. Management is the ability to achieve objectives with the resources available.

- Leadership – the influence. Leadership is the influencing of others to willingly follow.

They can be shown diagrammatically as in Figure 11.2.

Figure 11.2 The getting things done model

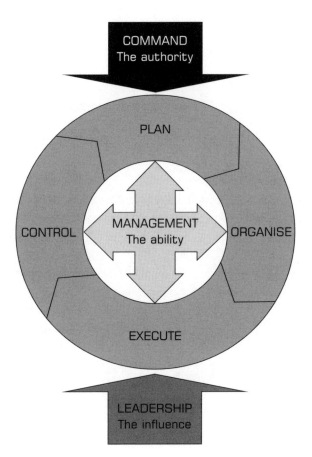

The Royal Navy ethos of being 'ready to fight and win' is its determination to achieve the aim, through whatever shape of formal leadership training that has been undertaken by the individuals within the service. ACL is a solid foundation of how the Royal Navy operates and manages to get things done. The Royal Navy also recognises what a potent and effective leadership tool ACL is. It is inherent in our development programmes, and our future leaders leave the Command Training Group understanding what benefits it can offer.

Task function

- Define the task.

- Make a plan.

- Briefing the group.

- Allocating work and resources.

- Controlling the quality and tempo of the work.

- Keeping informed of the progress in all areas.

- Checking team and individual performance against the plan.

- Adjusting the plan.

- Checking the aim has been achieved.

> "There are costs and risks to a programme of action. But they are far less than the long-range risks and costs of comfortable inactiveness."
>
> John F. Kennedy

Team function

- Involve the team in planning.

- Ensure that team members know each other's task.

- Set team standards and priorities.

- Appoint subleaders and maintain discipline.

- Maintain team spirit.

- Ensure communication within the team.

- Encourage and keep the team informed of progress.

- Training and developing the team.

> "It is that intangible force which will move a whole group of men to give their last ounce to achieve something without counting the cost to themselves; that makes them feel they are part of something greater than themselves."
>
> Field Marshall Sir William Slim

Individual function

- Attend to personal problems.

- Praise individuals.

- Encourage, reward and motivate.

- Provide a challenge.

- Recognise and use individual abilities.

- Respect others.

- Train and develop the individual.

- Every individual enjoys job satisfaction.

> "You can buy a man's time, you can buy his effort. But when you hand over his wage packet it contains nothing for enthusiasm, for self-respect or loyalty. These things the average man is ready to give freely in return for evidence that he personally counts, and the job he does is appreciated."
>
> Sir Bertram Waring

The heart of the three circles, the six functional skills of action-centred leadership

Naval leadership is visionary; it is the projection of personality and character to inspire and motivate sailors to do what is required of them, sometimes in difficult and dangerous situations. There is no prescription for leadership and no prescribed style of leader – the Royal Navy does not promote robots. Naval leadership is a combination of personal example, interpersonal skills, confidence, powers of persuasion and a compulsive will to achieve the aim. Leadership development in the Royal Navy transforms a person who has no or little concept of taking charge into a confident, adaptable and robust leader, having a thorough understanding of the needs of an individual and a balance of military qualities and professional skills. The successful military leader is an individual who understands his or her full capabilities and has a belief and pride in the organisation he or she represents. Leaders understand the environment in which they operate and, above all else, know the people that they lead and understand their needs.

Whatever formal leadership courses are undertaken by Royal Navy commissioned, non-commissioned officers or ratings, the students leave with the knowledge that will allow them to implement the three circles of ACL. The three-circle theory provides a structure, a base of knowledge, for the individuals to build upon in their ships. Additionally, with a clear understanding of the functional skills of ACL, which are the heart of the circles, students become more effective and confident when placed in a position of authority.

It is continually emphasised that the three circles are forever changing in size, depending on the situation. This all depends on the task to be achieved, the team activity and the needs of the participating individuals. It is the heart of the three circles, where they overlap, which provides the continuing leadership challenge.

Figure 11.3 The continuing leadership challenge

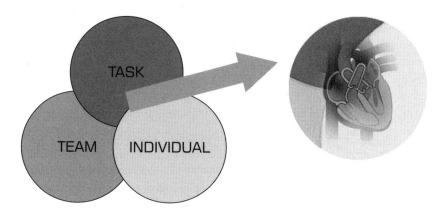

At CTG students are given many opportunities to put into practice the theories taught. These opportunities come in the form of directed command tasks, where students are put in syndicates and a leader nominated. The leader is then given an achievable task; additionally, certain restrictions about the task are explained and a set time frame is given. There are adequate resources available to enable the team to complete the task, but it is up to the leader to decide how to utilise the resources.

Leaders are formally assessed on their performance and their understanding of ACL, and how they transfer this knowledge from theoretical classroom session to the practical environment. Additionally, students are assessed on their presence, enthusiasm, problem-solving and decision-making capabilities, as well as their overall ability in planning, organising, along with the execution of their strategy and control of each team member's efforts.

Understanding the transferable functions of ACL is an essential element to the success of any task, and students are expected to:

- define the aim
- plan
- brief
- execute
- evaluate
- communicate.

Figure 11.4 The transferable functions of action-centred leadership

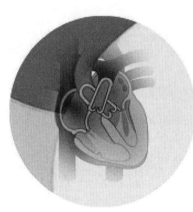

Furthermore, sincere encouragement and strong motivation are expected from the leader throughout all evolutions.

Defining the aim

- Identify the task and constraints.
- Involve the team.
- Share commitments and values.
- Clarify individual aims.
- Safety implications.

The planning

During the planning phase the leader:

- uses the SMART principle (specific – measurable – achievable – realistic – time bound)

- sets priorities, matching resources to the task

- listens to opinions

- considers options/contingencies

- assesses the individual's skills/competencies

- delegates, taking account of individual strengths and weaknesses

- sets targets and deadlines.

Briefing the plan

As leaders brief their plan, they are to:

- be clear and concise

- focus on a concrete solution

- ensure understanding from team members

- encourage questions

- be time-conscious.

The execution

While the plan is being executed the leader will:

- maintain standards

- quality control activities

- co-ordinate and control the team's efforts

- reconcile any conflicts.

Evaluation

As the plan is being executed, the leader will continuously evaluate the situation by:

- maintaining progress

- reviewing the aim and objectives

- re-planning and briefing as required

- recognising success and learning from mistakes.

Communication

The remaining link within the leader's circuit is that of communication, where the leader:

- clarifies the purpose

- may use a map, model or diagram to qualify the requirement

- achieves accuracy

- creates a communication that is logical

- creates a communication that is structured

- creates a communication that is sequential.

ACL and the Royal Navy

ACL and the functional, transferable skills work, without doubt. They are one of the most valued assets in the teaching of command, leadership and management which allows the Royal Navy to train its personnel to understand the concepts of how to 'get things done' so it is 'ready to fight and win'. Within the Royal Navy, the title 'superior officer' is not given lightly; it is a position of responsibility and accountability. This title is awarded to individuals who can adapt to a situation, react in a crisis, perform in adverse conditions and, above all, be decisive in action without hesitation and lead their people.

The Royal Navy fully endorses ACL and its leadership ethos. It encourages the individuals within the Service to know how they can further develop to become more effective and efficient leaders.

ACL remains one of the most valued leadership tools in the development doctrine of leadership training. ACL has guided Royal Navy leaders of the recent past and still inspirers officers and ratings, instilling a sense of honour, integrity, pride, enthusiasm, sense of belonging and the willingness to win.

"A leader is best when people scarcely know he exists. Not so good when they kindly obey and acclaim him. Worse when they despise him.

Fail to honour people, they fail to honour you. But of a good leader, who talks little, when his work is done and his aim fulfilled, they will say: 'We did this ourselves'.**"**

Lao-Tzu, 5th century BC – *Tao-Te Ching*

CASE STUDY 5

■ **ACTION-CENTRED LEADERSHIP IN THE ARMY**

Individual, team and task –these are three clearly understood principles in a military context when considering the art of leadership. Professor John Adair's identification of these three overlapping and inextricably linked functional needs has proved key components in leadership instruction in the Royal Military Academy Sandhurst for over three decades and continues to remain resonant and pertinent in today's military environment. While other approaches are also used to supplement Adair's theory, practical experience of leadership at all levels, in both a relatively benign staff environment and a more urgent and risk-filled operational deployment, reflects the enduring need to consider all three demands (often subconsciously) and identify the key element of the three in order to act as an effective leader.

The interaction of needs described by Adair continues to reflect the issues which must be considered by a leader in any situation in which he or she commands soldiers. Although we in the military operate in an increasingly sophisticated age in which technology plays a pervasive part, at the heart of what we do lies the need to lead people. Whether on increasingly frequent operational deployments or the simple routine of life in barracks, an officer's role remains immutable – to lead. Inherent within that role is the need for the leader to understand the often conflicting demands of completing a mission or task, ensuring that he or she has shaped the team and trained them to do so, while also taking into account, to some degree or other, the expectations of any one individual. Failure to balance these three needs leads to problems in one or all of the areas. This is why a fundamental appreciation of Adair's circles remains a key tenet of our early leadership training in Sandhurst. Indeed as leadership is seen in increasingly short supply in the world of business and industry, so it is increasingly important that one of the world's foremost centres of leadership training (and that is Sandhurst's principal role) fully understands the often conflicting elements which must be balanced in order to deliver effective leaders to the Field Army.

Adair's circles therefore still hold as true today as they did when he first wrote about them in his book *Training for leadership* in 1968. While nearly four decades may have passed, the core requirements of a leader have not changed. In that period, we have seen both a gradual emphasis away from the parade ground and three fundamental changes to the main course construction (from two years in length to 18 months, then down to six months and finally back up to one year). However, one area that has remained at the forefront of training has been an individual's ability to lead through careful examination of factors. That some of these factors are not labelled task, team and individual does not mean that they are not given due consideration in any assessment process where appropriate, but rather that they are implicit in every evaluation.

Theoretical leadership instruction at Sandhurst starts in the first term (in the initial 14 weeks), and soon addresses core concepts of theories of leadership, including Maslow's hierarchy of needs, Herzberg and needs and motivation, plus Blake and Mouton's managerial grid. These introduce officer cadets to a number of theories relevant to the military leader, along with the introduction of Adair's three circles.

The three circles therefore form a key element among a number of other well-proven and understood leadership theories which ensure that our future military leaders understand the concept of leadership in the round. In practical terms, after theoretical instruction, they then move on to command tasks which highlight quite clearly the conflicting demands of two out of three of these needs – notably task and team, with individual lying a distant though still present third.

In these 'command tasks', an individual is usually appointed as the team leader, and charged with completing a specific task, with limited resources in a set time. The task is always achievable, but difficult. The needs of the task always remain the same: a plan is required, the group needs to be briefed, work and resources need to be allocated, while quality control of the process is required throughout. Performance of the team must always be judged against the plan, with the plan adjusted where necessary, while always seeking to check progress against the aim. The requirement to fulfil these task-related needs never alters, either in structure or in sequence, with the better officer cadet quite clearly following this pattern while the less able individual tends to be less structured and more ad hoc in his or her approach. The more experienced a leader is in conducting command tasks, the more able that individual is to think about or consider the needs of his or her team.

Through experience of watching many hours of command tasks, it has become apparent that the more experienced a team leader is within the confines of the Academy, the more comfortable that person will be in involving the team in planning, setting tasks to individuals, coordinating the team's efforts, keeping their eye on the target through briefings: in other words most of the elements that constitute an understanding of the team's needs. Why is this so? It can largely be attributed to confidence in his or her team through common experience of the course gained up to that point. When the team leader and team itself (normally a 'section' of eight officer cadets) first tackles a command task, they are largely unfamiliar with the type of task they are trying to solve. The environment of Sandhurst is still new to them, while they are also uneasy in each other's company and do not know each other's strengths and weaknesses. As time progresses, these three elements change: they become more familiar with the type of task, if not the task itself, they are part of the military environment through immersion, while they know each other very well, each being forged in a common fashion through the fire of the Commissioning Course.

It is the *individual* element of the triumvirate of needs that it is probably most difficult to address within the milieu of a command task. Most of the needs simply do not apply to such a controlled environment. Individuals are generally well rested (or as well as they can be given the frenetic nature of the initial weeks of the course!), and their safety and security are not an issue. However, interestingly, self-esteem, achievement, ambition and personal interest do play a part in the relatively sterile world of the such an activity. If an individual has been tasked to play a part in the command task which is beyond his or her abilities (mostly physical, it must be said – such as breaching a gap that is too wide for that individual), and the team fails because of the leader's inappropriate choice of that person, then not only may the task be incomplete, but the team will also fail. Because the leader failed to choose the right individual, not only has the team failed, but the individual's self-esteem and confidence will also have taken a knock. Perhaps in this example paying too little attention to the selection of the right individual, while concurrently not taking into account his/her own desire to do well, could have quite an affect on all three needs – and perhaps the worst off here is the individual who feels he/she has let the team down, while also appearing less than able in front of the staff. Such a situation all too readily occurs as individuals get to know each other and their abilities within the testing environment of Sandhurst.

The example quoted above is perhaps rather a complex illustration of potentially conflicting needs which a leader needs to juggle in order to be effective. On operations, the situation can and usually is much more simple, encompassing the requirement to fulfil a mission or task set by a superior(s). One can take it as read that in this position the leader, the group and the individuals within that group are all well trained and prepared for their task – for example, a platoon patrol into Basra. The platoon commander will have received his (or her) mission which defines what is expected of him and what he has to achieve. There is a set procedure for the leader to develop a plan (known as the Estimate), and deliver it to his team (through the Orders process). Within those Orders he carefully defines what is to be done, by whom and when. During execution of the task, he will require situation reports from his subordinates, keeping him informed on their progress, while he will then adjust his plan as necessary in order to make it work. For example, if he finds his route blocked by a burning vehicle, then he will review options required to avoid such a position and resume his task. The platoon commander subconsciously (through experience and training) compares all these functions against his understanding of the aim of the task in order to assess to what extent his patrol is a success.

In such a situation, all the group needs revolve around the team being fully aware of their part in their commander's plan; where they have to be, when, doing what, and so on. The well-understood hierarchy within the military sees individuals with appropriate rank commanding their element in the platoon, working to the platoon commander. Through a clear and concise set of Orders they and their teams will know the plan and what they have to do within that plan. Throughout the operation, the platoon commander will brief downwards to the team leaders while they will also do so to their subordinates. Equally through the individual issue of the personal role radio, all ranks are in a position to pass information both upwards and downwards, ensuring a constant flow of information, helping to maintain situational awareness at all levels and at all times.

Debriefing after the patrol and incorporating the lessons learnt from its actions into training and preparation for future operations ensures that the team's needs are addressed almost in their entirety through a set of thoroughly understood and practised tactics, techniques and procedures.

As far as individual needs are concerned in the above example, often issues cannot be taken into overt consideration for operational reasons. For example, the tempo of an operation will dictate how much rest and sleep individuals receive, and in the high tempo of operations currently in Iraq, there is little doubt that on occasion rest will be at a premium. In terms of safety and security, much is provided through issued equipment such as body armour, but is not met by individuals requesting not to deploy because they are afraid of what they might face. Personal choice very much takes a back seat in such a situation. However, conversely an individual's esteem and self-fulfilment are almost always improved as a result of the experience he/she has gained through his/her time in an operational environment. People usually feel greater confidence and a real sense of achievement.

However, all the illustrations highlighted here are very much a spin-off from an enforced involvement in an operation, and are not based on personal choice. They have occurred as a direct result of being part of the team committed to the task. The fact that individuals have gained something from the operation and the overall deployment is a byproduct rather than an end in itself, although interestingly through self-fulfilment and a sense of achievement, allied to increasing effectiveness, the individual and the team benefit while the mission or task is invariably conducted more efficiently as a result.

The fact that Adair's circles are just about universally understood by all who have graduated from Sandhurst in the past 36 years must be regarded as something of a coup. They have outlasted most of the Commissioning Course, less drill, over that time. The fact that they remain relevant and pertinent both in the Academy and beyond is equally impressive, and is likely to see Adair's name remaining synonymous with Sandhurst for many more years to come.

CASE STUDY 6

■ LEADERSHIP DEVELOPMENT IN HIGHER EDUCATION

Background

Between 1990 and 2002, I had the unique opportunity of working with my friend and colleague, Dr Ron Schulz (now in retirement in Queensland, Australia), in developing and delivering the most comprehensive leadership development programme for higher education (HE) students in the United Kingdom.

The origins of this programme can be traced back to 1979 with John Adair's appointment as the world's first professor of leadership studies at the University of Surrey. In the late 1970s, John pioneered the introduction of action-centred leadership (ACL) training for undergraduate students, training which became embedded into the curriculum of many different disciplines including civil engineering. In 1986, Ron recruited the Civil Engineering Department to deliver the first two-day ACL training course for Level 2(1) students in chemical engineering, and in 1988 I was one of a small group of postgraduate student demonstrators who were trained to act as tutors on the Chemical Engineering Department's own version of the ACL course. By the time I joined the academic staff in 1990, Ron had already piloted a four-day advanced leadership training (ALT) course which was held in the Brecon Beacons, Wales; this course was run as a direct extension of the (by then) three-day ACL course.

Over the next eight years, we continually developed both the ACL and ALT courses, while additionally developing further elements of the programme. Additional skills training elements focusing on communication, teamworking and problem-solving, as a foundation for effective leadership development, were introduced in pre-university taster courses and embedded into the curriculum at Levels 1 and 2. At subsequent levels, the integration and application of leadership into technical and working environments was accomplished through professional training in industry and the integration of skills development into modules at Levels 3 and 4. Further embedding and understanding of leadership practice and development was accomplished by training Level 3 and 4 students to act as tutors on the ACL and ALT courses. Subsequently, graduates who had trained as leadership tutors brought their experiences of leadership practice in the workplace directly into our programme by delivering elements of our training courses. This involvement led to the instigation of the final element, the East African Projects, which focused on the development of operational leadership and management skills.

The leadership development programme

The development of our programme was an evolutionary process, and clearly the early participants only had the opportunity to undertake the elements available at the time. However, by 1998 all of the elements of the programme were in place. I have outlined the key components of the programme and some of the reasoning and drivers behind its development.

Foundation experience and development

The early elements of the programme were designed to provide a solid foundation on which to build leadership skills and experience, as well as providing students with their first exposure to a leadership role. Our pre-university taster courses in chemical engineering emphasised our belief that all engineers and scientists have a leadership role to perform in the workplace. Furthermore, they provided students with the opportunity of experiencing leadership, often for the first time, through taking on responsibility for leading a team operating a chemical plant. During the early stages of the degree programme students gained some experience of taking on a leadership role through working in teams in laboratory classes, and writing and presenting student workshops in technical modules. The importance of leadership skills in the workplace were also highlighted and developed in preparing students for securing their professional training placements.

Leadership training

The key elements of our leadership training were delivered in the latter half of Level 2; for the majority of our students this was immediately prior to undertaking their 12-month period of professional training. The centrepiece of the programme was a three-day ACL course delivered at the end of the academic year. This course was preceded by training in communication skills, including presentation skills and debating, teamworking and problem-solving skills.

The three-day ACL course focused on the three-circles concept and the principles of functional leadership, together with different satellite theories such as Maslow's needs hierarchy and Belbin's team roles. Students were divided into teams of six or seven, and each team was assigned a staff tutor and a student tutor (a Level 3 or 4 student who had been trained previously). The core material was delivered in short presentations which were followed by team/leadership tasks. All exercises were observed by the team tutors and individual team members, and on completion of the task the team tutors would lead a debrief of each task. Typically, over the three days, students would engage in at least 16 different tasks, with each individual taking on a leadership role and an observing role at least twice.

The ACL course was immediately followed by an optional advanced leadership training (ALT) course which was held in the Brecon Beacons, Wales; typically more than 60 per cent of the students would take up this option. On this course we were able to challenge our students with more demanding leadership tasks, an important aim of which was to provide them with the opportunity to really understand the needs of individuals, and their impact on a team and how it is led. However, we also wanted to create an environment in which the application of technical skills was essential. It took four years for this course to evolve into its final form; this was a six-day course culminating in a chemical weapons inspection scenario.

Over the first four days of the course the students engaged in a series of outdoor activities designed to test and develop their leadership, teamworking and communication skills. The first task involved getting the entire team (typically 20 students, although at its height we had 28) to a particular location in Wales, by a specific time while accomplishing other, smaller tasks on the way. Subsequent outdoor activities included obstacle courses, terrain-crossing skills, river crossings and a trial chemical weapons inspection. However, the first part of the course was all preparation for the final two days, during which the students would undertake a real chemical weapons inspection on a mobile chemical facility.

The preparation and planning phase for the real inspection would typically take between 16 and 20 hours, while the inspection itself would last no longer than four hours. The team of students, led by one of their peers, would have to devise a detailed team structure, with subleaders at all levels, learn how to use specialist inspection equipment, devise detailed plans for each aspect of the actual inspection, and plan how they were to interact with the plant owners and operators. To achieve this we enlisted the help of our graduates, some of whom by then were ex-chemical weapons inspectors themselves, to coach and assist the students during the preparation and planning phase. Ultimately, however, the students would have to take on the inspection themselves, and deliver a preliminary report, all within seven hours. We ran this scenario successfully for 10 years, developing the detail and realism of the task as we fostered links with the world's international chemical weapons inspection community.

Application and integration of leadership in chemical engineering

One of the early problems we encountered when we introduced leadership training into the curriculum was the tendency of students to pigeonhole the experience and learning, and consequently not apply it effectively on their professional training placements or their academic/technical work. We overcame the first problem with the addition of two elements to the programme. First, we started training student volunteers, at Levels 3 and 4, to become student tutors for the delivery of the ACL and ALT courses. All students undertook a day's training which focused on the observing and debriefing of leadership tasks, and supporting the delivery of the more complex aspects of these courses. This opportunity was so popular that we often had student teams with two or even three student tutors on the ACL course. Second, we introduced the review of leadership, and other skills, explicitly into our programme for monitoring students' progress in industry when visiting them on their professional training placement.

The second problem had its roots in transferability. I can clearly remember a discussion with a group of students who were having problems with their design project. When I asked who was taking on the leadership role in the team, they replied that no one had told them that this was a leadership exercise! Our immediate solution to this problem was to directly overcome this issue during the ACL and ALT courses. We did this first, by raising students' awareness of how these skills could be applied to their academic/technical studies, and second, through encouraging the student tutors to relate their own experiences of applying these skills during their studies. Furthermore, we also introduced a tutoring system for the design projects, which focused on leadership and team working problems specifically.

However, to address the problem of transferability most effectively, we identified the need for a new module to be introduced into the curriculum, which would directly highlight the need for and integrate the use of technical, academic and personal skills, particularly leadership, in a chemical engineering environment. To some extent, we had already achieved this through the use of the chemical weapons inspection scenario on the ALT course, but we believed that something more mainstream was required. The module we designed focused on operating a chemical plant, an environment in which the application of technical and academic skills was essential, but no more so than the effective application of communication, teamworking, problem-solving and, above all, leadership skills.

This was a major undertaking which required the design and construction of a small-scale production plant and control room, as well as the development of new teaching and training materials. Esso initially funded the project with £10,000 through its Higher Education Support Scheme, and the university itself provided further funding for the three-year project. Ultimately, we achieved much more than we set out to do. The outcome was a comprehensive teaching framework which could effectively demonstrate the need for leadership skills in the chemical engineering environment, as well as many other technical, academic and personal skills. This teaching framework has now been used at all levels, from exposing A-level students to a chemical engineering environment to training prospective international chemical weapons inspectors.

Advanced leadership development

As the programme matured, we built up a substantial group of graduate alumni who were eager to continue to support the programme. A number of these graduates contributed directly to the development and delivery of both the ACL and ALT courses: suggesting improvements and additions based upon their own experiences, running their own training sessions and taking on different roles in support of our scenarios. However, it also became clear that these graduates had a real desire for further leadership development.

In July 1995, the first team of graduates on the East African Project arrived in Nairobi. These graduates had spent the previous six months working part-time preparing for a three-week stay in East Africa. They had been tasked two main projects: the design, construction and commissioning of a pilot-scale, field-based essential oils distillation unit, which was to be tested on the Ol Ari Nyiro Ranch in Laikipia, northern Kenya; and the technical evaluation and modification of a production-scale essential oils plant in Arusha, Tanzania. Each of the participants had had to raise £1,600 and secure three weeks' leave from his or her company (ICI, BP and Shell). The project was planned and carried out entirely by the team, which had control of all aspects of the project including the project finances. We simply provided logistical and health and safety back-up.

This project proved to be a real test of personal, team and operational leadership. The distillation unit testing in Laikipia was carried out in the field, literally! This required the sourcing and provision of tented accommodation, food and equipment (technical and domestic) for the entire team, which also included four student trainees from the University of Nairobi; the planning and preparation for transporting this equipment over 400 kilometres across the Great Rift Valley; and the organisation and management of the testing site, with emphasis being placed on health, safety and environmental issues, as well as domestic arrangements. In addition to these considerations, the team had to build and commission the distillation unit, train the university students to operate and maintain the unit, and produce a suitably pure sample of essential oils distillate for analysis by a major international company.

The second project involved transporting the main project team over 700 kilometres to Arusha in northern Tanzania. They then had the responsibility of making major process modifications to an operational production facility in order to optimise the process performance within 48 hours.

The project debrief was a splendid affair, sundowners in Tarangire National Park. I clearly remember realising that we had completed our contribution to the leadership development journey of these individuals, when Jerry Conlon of Shell pulled out his three-circles leadership card, which he must have carried around with him for the best part of eight years, and announced that he no longer needed it because it had become instinctive.

Three more East African Projects followed in 1997, 1999 and 2001. All followed a similar format, but larger project teams allowed us to take on more individual projects. Essential oils were a recurring theme, but the teams also undertook environmental projects, large-scale process optimisation projects, terrain mapping, and of course they delivered leadership training courses to local industry.

Our motivation

Given that both Ron and I were academics in technical disciplines, both with active and growing research groups and burgeoning administrative commitments, one of the most common questions we have been asked is what motivated us to undertake the development and delivery of this programme. As is often the case, our motivation was a combination of different drivers: in this case pragmatism, opportunity and inspiration.

Initially, we had a real need to provide our students with a distinct advantage over their contemporaries in the securing of jobs for professional training placements and on graduation. Training in leadership skills had an immediate and significant impact on the ease with which our students could secure interviews and job offers, but even more noticeable was the quality of the organisations that wished to employ them. Although Surrey was not regarded as a target university by companies such as ICI or BP, the chemical engineering department was singled out and specifically targeted, receiving annual visits for both student and graduate recruitment drives.

Our initial successes were extremely well received by both students and employers. It became clear that students would relish the opportunity for further leadership development, and that we could get support and financial assistance from employers to generate these opportunities. Furthermore, we quickly recognised that we were in a unique position with respect to leadership development. We had the opportunity to design a comprehensive programme which could span the entire four years of the degree programme, have a real developmental thread and become integrated into the core academic curriculum. This was an opportunity we could not turn down.

Ultimately, however, our motivation to develop the more adventurous and challenging aspects of the programme came from the successes of our graduates. We quickly realised that we were inspiring the young people to achieve things that they initially did not think they would be capable of. Even more importantly, we immediately saw the benefit of designing our programme to directly draw on this experience, as much as anything because we were inspired by what they had achieved. In essence, and I quote this often: *We inspired people to do great things, they inspired us to inspire others.*

Outcomes and achievements

There have been many individual success stories which have been a direct result of students' and graduates' participation and involvement in the development of this programme. However, we have also influenced a large number of people. Between 1986, when we first introduced the ACL programme to chemical engineering, and 2002 when I left Surrey, over 800 students had completed the ACL course and the elements leading up to it, almost 300 students had completed the ALT course in Brecon, and 30 graduates had undertaken the East African projects.

There have also been some unusual spin-offs. Most notably as a direct result of our ALT course in Brecon, 12 graduates from the department were seconded to the United Nations through the Foreign and Commonwealth Office to work as biological and chemical weapons inspectors for UNSCOM, the United Nations Special Commission to Iraq. All these individuals took on leadership roles during inspection activities. In addition, Ron and I now deliver a high-profile training programme for prospective chemical weapons inspectors, with the development of leadership and business management skills at its core, for the Organisation for the Prohibition of Chemicals Weapons in The Hague.

From a personal perspective, Ron and I received a lot of recognition for our achievements, through numerous awards and prizes. Most notably for me, this was being awarded the inaugural Frank Morton Medal for Teaching Excellence in Chemical Engineering. This programme featured heavily in my submission and public lecture.

Dr David Faraday CEng MIChemE ILTM
evolve LEADTEAM Ltd

CASE STUDY 7

IMPERIAL CHEMICAL INDUSTRIES (ICI)

"We must obey the greatest law of change. It is the most powerful law of nature."

Edmund Burke

This case study is now more than a quarter of a century old, but I have included it because it is a classic of how a commercial organisation first applied the practical philosophy associated with my name.

In September 1981 Bill Stead and Edgar Vincent – the two senior managers responsible for group personnel in ICI – came to see me at the University of Surrey. They gave me some background about the plight of ICI – 1980 had been a disastrous year in which profits fell by 48 per cent and the dividend was cut for the first time since formation in 1926 – and told me that the executive directors had decided that the first priority in personnel strategy should be the development of what they called manager-leaders. They wished me to act as an outside consultant.

My previous contacts with ICI had been few and far between. In the 1970s I knew it from afar as a company that had spent hundreds of thousands of pounds on hiring behavioural scientists, mainly American and some most distinguished, such as Douglas McGregor. Some innovations, for example the work on job enrichment, had had a high profile. It had a reputation for sophistication in its various management systems and management development programmes. Through the agency of the Chemical and Allied Products Industrial Training Board in the 1970s I spent a few days at ICI's ammonia plant on Teesside as co-trainer on a course for supervisors. That was about the sum of my knowledge.

Edgar Vincent asked me if I could suggest other organisations that had used my ideas to grow leaders, except the Army which he and his colleague had already visited.

I remember being stuck for an answer. There were of course many organisations – some 2000 of them in 1981 – that were sending managers and supervisors on ACL courses, or even putting the whole management though an ACL programme, but that was not the question put to me. I could think of no organisations that were *growing* leaders in the ways I had been recommending. I suggested that ICI might like to be the first real guinea-pig, and the pair of them thought that would be an excellent idea. They also suggested that in exchange such a project should prove an extremely valuable opportunity in the context of my own research into leadership and leadership development.

After some further discussions with Edgar, now group personnel manager, we agreed on a plan to get the ball rolling. Instead of writing a paper on strategy or the board issuing a set of edicts, it was decided that a major conference would be convened at Warren House, ICI's conference centre, at which a cross-section of able top managers in ICI's nine divisions could meet and discuss the matter, hearing from various specialists like me in the course of three days. Then it would be left up to them to identify the right strategy for ICI, and for their own divisions within it, in order to achieve the first of ICI's key personnel policies – the development of management-leaders.

The Warren House conference

The Warren House conference took place in January 1982, based on a programme that Edgar and I had worked out together. As consultant I was present throughout. I also gave one talk about the functional approach to leadership, together with some reminders about the contribution of Maslow and Herzberg, and the importance of understanding the decision-making continuum. Apart from the personnel director and chairman of ICI, the other speakers were Peter Prior (chairman of Bulmers), David Gilbert-Smith (Leadership Trust), and Andrew Stewart (a psychologist and independent management consultant who spoke about methods of selecting or assessing leaders).

Since my initial meeting with Edgar and his colleague, ICI had appointed in November a new chairman from among its three deputy chairmen – not the one who had been mentioned to me as the most likely. Edgar evidently regarded his appointment as a considerable bonus to the enterprise of leadership development that we were engaged upon. I met John Harvey-Jones for the first time in the bar at Warren House that evening (27 January) and he spoke to the conference informally after supper.

The chairman began by saying that ICI was wrongly positioned in terms of where its hardware was, its types of products, and its overcapacity in some areas. Above all it was not well positioned in the real growth markets of the Far East and the United

States. This picture had implications for management style and leadership pattern. 'We have first-class management,' he said, 'but it has become excessively bureaucratic and political. We've adopted a value system that is ponderous, negative, unanxious to share risk and not willing to give headroom.

'What's the pattern for the next ten years? Instability and change will characterise it. It will be a repositioning decade, with lots of new patterns and shifts of power. Growth, as we've known it, will be greatly reduced. No company can exist without growth, therefore we have to make it by pinching the markets of competitors, outdating his products and developing new ones,' John Harvey-Jones continued. He talked some more about how he saw the emergence of some giants in the chemicals industry in Europe, a pattern like the one in America. Technologically we were in for enormous change.

'What do we need to work in this environment?' he next asked. 'A new attitude to risk – we minimise risk, we don't maximise opportunities. But the biggest risk of all is to take no risk. We have to be flexible, because we won't read the future right. We need to have an ability to move fast, more market sensitivity, more openness and trust, greater tolerance of differences and more courage in dealings with others. Individuals have the answers, not ICI as a group.'

John Harvey-Jones then turned to his work plans after he became formally chairman in April. He would start at the top with the board. 'Let's meet in the middle. We haven't got time for a slow trickle-down.' Double-guessing would be cut out by having fewer people – the size of the board would be reduced for a start. The discussion that followed was exceptionally frank on all sides. In response to one question the chairman pointed to 'the catalytic things we can do' to encourage entrepreneurial enterprise. 'The present ICI system will kill any business! The dynamic has been increasingly centralised. One of my jobs at every level has been to hold an umbrella over my chaps' heads. Senior management is about getting people to own the problem and to do something about it, not passing it up. Our system must be not to have a system.'

A sense of urgency coloured his closing remarks. It is a race against time – we are too late – the world is breaking up – bits to be grabbed now. His vision was of an adaptable, open, flexible, fast-moving ICI – ready to move quickly in perceived thrusts or directions. 'We've got to grow this new ICI.' Asked about the attitude of his fellow directors he said that he couldn't order them. 'I have to lead the board to lead. They voted for me. There is no such thing as one leader. What matters most is a common sense of values. Leadership is about getting extraordinary performance out of ordinary people. In ICI we have got extraordinary people to begin with.'

In answer to another question John Harvey-Jones highlighted another strength. 'ICI exists through its ability to work informal systems. We have got the ability to work together informally. I'm keen on clarity of organizational responsibilities, but we've got to keep this informal ability to work together, because we'll never get the structure right. We start miles ahead of any other European chemical company; we have shown in the last two years that we can be unbelievably fast. We've got a lot going for us, such as a good technological basis. In other respects I could wish we were better placed. But we can knock the hell out of the opposition.'

Inspired by those words and determined to end the 'treacle', as they called it, which the ICI bureaucratic culture had created, the participants in the conference continued working all next day on their strategic action plans for liberating the leadership and enterprise within ICI.

Leadership training in ICI

Among the recommendations, each of the nine divisional teams resolved to introduce leadership training based upon the three-circles approach – task, team and individual – that I had outlined. In keeping with the new emphasis on decentralisation, it was left to the divisions to devise their own leadership training programmes, using me as a resource. My contribution varied accordingly. Looking through my diaries I see that I spoke to all the senior managers in one division; spent three days at Warren House with all the finance directors and their teams; advised one division on its leadership course, and did some on the spot 'training of the trainers' after the first one; did some counselling sessions with some divisional directors on an individual basis; advised four managers who had been asked to make recommendation on the key issue of leadership to the board of Organics Division; reviewed ICI's methods of selecting graduates; and carried out an evaluation survey of all the external leadership courses currently being used by ICI. But perhaps my most important contribution was to lead a one-day seminar each year for four years with Edgar Vincent for the nine divisional training managers responsible for the functional leadership courses in their various forms.

It is not within my compass here to say more about the radical changes that have taken place during the chairmanship of Sir John Harvey-Jones, which ended in 1987, especially as Sir John himself is writing a book on the subject. As I mentioned earlier, in 1984 ICI was the first company to break the £1 billion profit barrier (the second, National Westminster Bank, has also made continual use of ACL since its introduction in 1969).

Of course the success of ICI in the period under review cannot be ascribed entirely to leadership, although I don't suppose that anyone would deny the importance of leadership as shown by Sir John Harvey-Jones and by many other ICI manager-leaders at every level in the divisions. As for leadership development, all that can be safely said is that it has proved to be not incompatible with business success.

> "Leadership is about getting extraordinary performance out of ordinary people."
>
> Sir John Harvey-Jones

Later, having fended off a hostile take-over bid from Lord Hanson, ICI split into two: Astra Zeneca and Centrica. Astra Zeneca has recently been singled out as one of the top 10 companies in Europe that is both financially successful and dedicated to a strategy of leadership development. The tradition lives on.

Key points

- In 1981 the board of ICI accepted a key personnel strategy as part of its overall business strategy of repositioning and regenerating ICI. (The personnel director is one of the seven or eight directors on the main board.) That overall strategy has been successful: ICI is back among the world leaders in the chemical and pharmaceutical industries. 'Just as we need a business vision for the future we need a people vision too,' said Harvey-Jones in 1982 to the representatives of ICI's employees. Good selection procedure has ensured that ICI had a good supply of actual and potential manager-leaders.

- The main thrust of the new programmes in leadership training for managers and supervisors came within the nine divisions. All these programmes used the three-circles model as the basis of their teaching about good leadership in management.

- Like all large companies ICI had faced the problem that divisions tended not to release people for career development purposes. However, it made substantial progress in that direction.

- The importance is stressed of managers knowing their people as individuals, dealing with them face to face and getting their support.

- A small 'research and advisory' team – the group personnel manager and his divisional counterparts – guided the leadership training programme.

- Layers of hierarchy and scores of committees were scythed away in the division and at headquarters, where Harvey-Jones dispensed with two deputy chairmen and reduced the size of the main board. One divisional board was reduced from 20 directors to six. A rigorous policy of decentralizing decision-making authority and central services, such as purchasing and shipping, was followed.

- Much more emphasis was put on individuals using their own initiative and 'owning' their own self-development.

- In the 1970s ICI suffered from the problems of size. According to a senior ICI man 'It employed too many high-paid people to check and cross-check other men's figures. It was an over-educated company. It had a technical bias, was not breeding people with entrepreneurial flair.' A new organisational climate has begun to emerge in which leadership can grow and flourish. The chairman's role was strengthened into that of chief executive (called 'principal executive officer' in ICI). As tenant of it, Sir John Harvey-Jones not only showed leadership by giving the company a sense of direction – 'I hope I am a leader but I'm not a one-man band' – but did all in his power to encourage it in others. He talked about it, placing it high in his list of values. He took part in training courses, and in one year met more than 8,000 ICI managers in group discussions.

> **"**How do you know you have won? When the energy is coming the other way and when your people are visibly growing individually and as a group.**"**
>
> Sir John Harvey-Jones

PARTING THOUGHTS

When I wrote the world's first book on leadership development in 1968 – *Training for leadership* – organisational life was rather different. Then there were many trainers employed directly by large corporations and the public services. But that world has changed. Training departments, for example, have shrunk dramatically in size or disappeared, and many organisations tend now – for better or worse – to out-source their training requirements to a whole range of suppliers.

Not that those corporate training departments were very good at bringing about change. They could run courses – in the 1970s there were hundreds of ACL courses – but organisational culture was not on the agenda. In those days, anyway, leadership was see as merely a small part of the bigger picture of management, and the high temples of management were the new business schools of the 1960s.

What broke the mould of old-style management was change – economic, technological, information, social, educational change. It was, of course, a universal phenomenon. Living in the same global village, facing ever more severe global competition, organisations found themselves gripped in the turbulence of change. And, as I have said, change throws up the need for leaders, and leaders bring about desirable change. Hence, one of the great intellectual revolutions of our times has been the fall of the old-style manager and the rise of the business leader. It is comparable to the fall of Communism. Indeed the two phenomena are linked, for, as I have said above, Communism was old-style managerialism – planning and controlling the whole economy – carried to excess. It did not work.

Just as pride often precedes a fall, however, so do great expectations often lead to great disappointments. And the disappointment of cherished hopes is a fertile swamp or breeding ground for despair and cynicism, those diseases of the human spirit. One of my major concerns, as the world's principal adviser on leadership development, has been that the contemporary emphasis on leadership, the constant and often mindless repetition of the word, and the rise of leadership courses, centres, colleges and foundations, will all create false expectations. For they are often castles built on the sands of speculative theories, unsound concepts and get-rich-quick marketing strategies. To avoid massive disappointment and cynicism, we in the leadership field have to demonstrate that leadership development is not just old management development under the new and sexy name of leadership. Above all we have to show that it really does work.

It may be beyond my power to prevent the tidal waves of disappointment that are going to hit the leadership industry in the next two or three years, especially in America. What I can do, however, is to help you to ensure that your organisation roots its leadership development programme in a solid and tested foundation of experience. Then it will bear fruit year-on-year. By 'fruit' I mean managers or their equivalents who really do enable others to achieve challenging tasks, who build teams and who motivate and inspire individuals. By growing the business, they grow people – and they themselves grow in the process.

In this book I have stressed the fact that the person who owns the problem of leadership development in an organisation is the strategic leader – the chief executive or equivalent. But this does not mean that they have to do it all themselves. That would be impossible, for it is only one of the seven generic functions of a strategic leader. So what all organisations need is a specialist manager (staff rather than line) in the field of leadership development. For everything in this field depends on a great partnership between chief executive and specialist – think, as an example, of Sir John Harvey-Jones and Edgar Vincent in the ICI case study (Part 3).

In a large organisation, that specialist may be the Director of Human Resources, or perhaps a senior colleague in that department. But if the HR function gets reduced in size, then HR managers are constrained to be ever more the generalist. Therefore I can see the need for really professional independent leadership development advisers (I do not call them consultants, though that is what they are) who will work directly with the chief executive and the HR director or manager to help them formulate, implement and sustain a successful leadership development strategy tailored to the specific needs of their organisation. This is the role I have myself played in ICI, Exxon Chemicals, British Rail, Hambros and others. Now – not least as a result of this book – it may be your turn. All my trade secrets are here for you!

A last word. Remember that leadership development at any level is not simply about equipping leaders or would-be leaders with knowledge and skills. You are there to inspire them too. Your own enthusiasm, commitment and example will go a long way down that road. But the true secret of inspiration for a teacher as well as a leader begins when you sense the greatness that lies in others. It is our immense privilege to play a part in releasing that greatness. Heaven knows, the world stands in need of good leaders and teachers for good, those who will stir up the greatness of others.

Thank you for sharing the journey of this book with me. I hope it may serve you as both guidebook and friend upon the journey that lies ahead of you. My thoughts go with you.

■ APPENDIX

■ LIST OF BASIC LEADERSHIP FUNCTIONS

Planning

Seeking all available information

Defining group task, purpose or goal

Making a workable plan (in right decision-making framework).

Initiating

Briefing group on the aims and the plan

Explaining why aim or plan is necessary

Allocating tasks to group members

Setting group standards.

Controlling

Maintaining group standards

Influencing tempo

Ensuring all actions are taken towards objectives

Keeping discussion relevant

Prodding group to action/decision.

Supporting

Expressing acceptance of persons and their contribution

Encouraging group/individuals

Disciplining group/individuals

Creating team spirit

Relieving tension with humour

Reconciling disagreements or getting others to explore them.

Informing

Clarifying task and plan

Giving new information to the group (keeping them in the picture)

Receiving information from the group

Summarising suggestions and ideas coherently.

Evaluating

Checking feasibility of an idea

Testing the consequences of a proposed solution

Evaluating group performance

Helping the group to evaluate its own performance against standards.

■ NOTES

▢ 2 THE NATURE OF LEADERSHIP

1   Bird and Appleton (1940, pp 378–379). Professor Bird of the University of Minnesota looked at approximately 20 studies 'bearing some resemblance to controlled investigations' which contained 79 traits:

> Surprisingly little overlapping is found from study to study. Actually, 51 or 65 per cent, are mentioned once, 16 or 20 per cent are common to two lists, 4 or 5 per cent are found in three, and another 5 per cent in four lists. Two traits are common to five lists, and one trait, namely initiative, to six, and another one, high intelligence, to ten lists.
>
> (Bird and Appleton 1940, p379)

2   The diagram appears in Canadian Armed Forces (1960).

3   On the subject of motivation, closely related to the satisfaction of individual needs in work, the research work of F. Herzberg, professor of psychology at Western Reserve University, USA, and his associates is highly relevant. See Herzberg, Mausner and Snyderman (1959) and Herzberg (1966). For a full discussion of Maslow, Herzberg, Douglas McGregor, Rensis Likert and other theorists on motivation, see my *Understanding motivation* (Adair 1989) and *Effective motivation* (Adair 1998).

■ REFERENCES

ADAIR, J. (1968) *Training for leadership*

ADAIR, J. (1969) *Training for decisions*

ADAIR, J. (1973a) *Action-centred leadership*

ADAIR, J. (1973b) *Training for communication*

ADAIR, J. (1974) *Management and morality: some problems and opportunities of social capitalism*

ADAIR, J. (1983) *Effective leadership*

ADAIR, J. (1988) *Developing leaders*

ADAIR, J. (1989) *Understanding motivation*

ADAIR, J. (1998) *Effective motivation*

ADAIR, J. (2001) *Effective strategic leadership*

ALLPORT, G.W. and ODBERT, H.A. (1936) Trait-names: a psycholexical study, *Psychological Monographs*, No. 211.

BIRD, C. and APPLETON, D. (1940) *Social psychology,* New York and London: Wiley.

CANADIAN ARMED FORCES. (1960) *Leadership for the professional officer*, Toronto: CFP 131 (2).

Council for Excellence in Management and Leadership (2001) *Report on best-practice leadership development*. www.managementandleadershipcouncil.org\pubmain.htm (accessed on 12 September 2005).

COVEY, S.R. (1992) *Principle-centred leadership*, London: Simon and Schuster.

GIBB, C.A. (1954) Leadership. In G. Lindzey (ed), *Handbook of social psychology*, Vol. 2.

GLEICK, J. (1992) *Genius: Richard Feynman and modern physics*, London: Little Brown.

GOLEMAN, D. (1998) *Working with emotional intelligence*, London: Bloomsbury.

GRINT, K. (2004) *What is leadership?* Working paper, Said Business School and Templeton College, Oxford University.

HERZBERG, F. (1966) *Work and the nature of man*, Cleveland: World Publishing.

HERZBERG, F., MAUSNER B. and SNYDERMAN, B.B. (1959) *The motivation to work,* 2nd edn, New York: Wiley.

HOOPER, R.A. and POTTER, J.R. (1997) *The business of leadership*, Aldershot: Ashgate.

JENKINS, W.O. (1947) A review of leadership studies with particular reference to military problems, *Psychological Bulletin*, No. 44, pp 54–79.

LANYON, R. I. and GOODSTEIN, L. (1997) *Personality assessment*, 3rd edn, Chichester: Wiley.

MASLOW, A.H. (1954) *Motivation and personality,* New York: Harper.

MATTHEWS, G., DEARY, I.J. and WHITEMAN, M. C. (2003) *Personality traits*, 2nd edn, New York: Harper.

MONTGOMERY, FIELD MARSHAL VISCOUNT. (1961) *The path to leadership*, London: Collins.

POPPER, K. (1976) *Unended quest*, London: Collins.

REECE, I. and WALKER, S. (1992) *Teaching, training and learning*, Sunderland: Business Education Publishers.

ROYAL AIR FORCE (2003) *Developing excellence in leadership*

STOGDILL, R.M. (1948) Personal factors associated with leadership: a survey of the literature, *Journal of Psychology*, Vol. 25, pp35–71.

STOREY, J. (2004) *Leadership in organisations*, London: Routledge

TANNENBAUM, R. and SCHMIDT, W.H. (1958) How to choose a leadership pattern, *Harvard Business Review*, March–April.

TEAD, O. (1935) *The art of leadership*, New York: Addison-Wellesly.

INDEX

A

action-centred leadership *see* leadership
action plans 40, 42, 117, 148
Adair, John 23, 32, 33, 34, 67, 97, 111,
     112, 114, 116, 120, 131, 132, 135,
     137, 157
Adam, Sir Ronald 54
Alexander the Great 92
Allan, William 109
Allport, G. W. 9
Amazon.com 111
Appleton, D. 157
Astra Zeneca 149
Athena 83, 85, 88
Augustine, Saint 86, 90
Avanessian, Stepan 115

B

Barnard, Chester 83
Belbin, R. 139
"big six" functional leadership process
     120
Bird, C. 157
Blake, R. 132
Blanchard, K. 109, 114

Britannia Royal Naval College (BRNC)
     119–20
British Army 6, 34, 54
British Institute of Directors 97
British Rail 152
Bulmers 146
Burke, Edmund 90, 145

C

Caesar, Julius 92
Callaghan, James (Lord Callaghan) 98
Cameron, Sir Neil 34
Carnegie, Andrew 84
case studies
     1: Action-centred leadership in the
          Scottish police 107–10
     2: RAF use of action-centred
          leadership 111–14
     3: Action-centred leadership in
          Armenia 115–18
     4: Royal Navy leadership training and
          action-centred leadership
          119–30
     5: Action-centred leadership in the
          army 131–5

6: Leadership development in higher
    education 137–43
7: ICI 145–50
Centre for Leadership Development (CLD)
    115–18
Centrica 149
CEO 43, 48
Chaucer, Geoffrey 91, 94
Chester, Barry 116
Churchill, Sir Winston 17, 90
Cicero 92
Cincinnatus 96
CIPD 23
Collier, John 4
Collingwood, Admiral 46
Comino, Dmitri 57
Conlon, Jerry 142
Covey, Stephen 114
Crick, F. 8

D
Deary, I. J. 56
Degnan, Kenny 109
Dickens, Charles 82
Drucker, Peter 29, 89
Dulverton Trust 34

E
Ecclesiastes 95
Einstein, A. 7, 25, 71
Eisenhower, President Dwight D. 79
Enron 45
Euripides 45
Exxon Chemicals 152

F
Falk, Roger 43
Faraday, David 143

Feather, Vic 3
Feynman, Richard 24
Fitzgerald, Frances 5
functional approach *see* leadership
functional leadership *see* leadership

G
Gaius Antonius 53, 54
Galba 56
General Motors 77
Gibb, C. A. 21
Gilbert-Smith, David 146
Gleick, James 24
Goethe, Johann Wolfgang 88, 101
Gogbashian, Alan 115
Goleman, Daniel 114
Goodstein, L. 56
Grant, President Ulysses S. 96
Grint, K. 111

H
Hambros 152
Hannibal 92, 95
Hanson, Lord 149
Harvard Business Review 17, 24
Harvard Business School 34
Harvey-Jones, Sir John 146–52
Hersey, P. 109, 114
Herzberg, F. 116, 132, 146, 157
Hildreth, Jan 97
HMS Collingswood 120
HMS Royal Arthur 121
Hooper, R. A. 114

I
Imperial Chemical Industries (ICI) 39, 98,
    141, 142, 145–50, 152
Internet 24, 65

J
Jagger, Dean 108
Jones, Wendy 109
Jupp, John 114

K
Kennedy, President John F. 17, 124

L
Lanyon, R. I. 56
Lao-Tzu 130
Lawrence, T. E. 7
leadership
    action-centred leadership (ACL) 6,
        34, 64, 67, 68, 105–50
    advanced leadership training (ALT)
        137–43
    career development 73–82
        and equal opportunities 79–80
        hourglass model of 75–6
        planning principles 77–9
    and the chief executive 96–8
    and corporate culture 98
    development 23–36
        corporate culture for 89–90
        importance of books 91–2
        natural system of 46–7
        obstacles to 47–9
        self-development 89–94
        seven principles of 37–42
        strategy for 43–52
    difference from management 26–9,
        49–50
    functional approach 12–17, 111, 114,
        116, 146
    functional leadership 6, 7, 21, 29,
        32–4, 55, 64, 67, 68, 90, 120,
        138, 148

levels of 30–3, 68–9
mentors 83–8
    development of 84–6
nature of 5–22
operational leadership 46, 47, 55, 56,
    57, 68, 70, 114, 138, 141
qualities approach 9–11
responsibility 16, 30–1, 57
sharing 17–21
situational approach 11–12
strategic leadership 33, 39, 43, 46,
    47, 53, 55, 56, 67, 69, 75, 76,
    79, 80, 86, 90, 95–101, 152
training for 34–6, 61–71
    outdoor/experiential 67–8
Lee, Robert E. 95
Lego 67, 108
Likert, Rensis 157
Lincoln, Abraham 96

M
Manhattan Project 63
Mant, Alistair 60
Maslow, A. H. 14, 116, 132, 138, 146,
    157
Matsushita, Konosuke 34–5
Matthews, G. 56
Mausner, B. 157
Maxwell, Robert 45
MBA 28–9
McGregor, Douglas 34, 145,
    157
Mentor 83
mentors *see* leadership
Merrill, Gary 108
Minnesota 157
Mitsubishi Corporation 116
Mogg, Sir John 34

Montgomery, Field Marshal Viscount 31, 32, 44, 58
Morton, Frank 143
Mouton, J. 132

N
National Health Service (NHS) 10, 16, 48, 49, 50, 62
National Westminster Bank 148
NCOs 32, 114, 120, 121, 122
needs
    circles of 15
    hierarchy of 15
    individual 14–20, 31, 132–4, 139, 157
    task 13, 17, 31, 132–4
    team/group 13–17, 31, 132–4
    see also Maslow, A. H.
Nelson, Horatio Lord 23, 46

O
Odbert, H. A. 9
Odysseus 83
operational leadership *see* leadership

P
Peck, Gregory 108
Penelope 83
Perkins, Dorothy 34
"Peter Principle" 33, 71
Plutarch 53
Popper, Sir Karl 24
Potter, J. R. 114
Prior, Peter 146
Prudential 34

Q
qualities approach *see* leadership

R
Reece, I. 114
Royal Air Force 6, 12, 34, 111, 112, 113, 114
Royal Air Force College Cranwell 111–13
Royal College of Nursing 67
Royal Navy 6, 12, 119, 121, 123, 125, 129
Royal United Services Institute 34
Ryle, Gilbert 5

S
Sandhurst 6, 23, 34, 55, 58, 62, 67, 131, 132, 133, 135
Schmidt, W. H. 17, 24, 116
Schulz, Ron 137, 142, 143
Schweitzer, Albert 99
Scipio Africanus 92, 96
Scott, Thomas A. 84
Scottish Police College, The 107–10
selection 53–60
    of business leaders 56–7
    psychological testing in 56
    of team leaders 54–5
Shakespeare, William 73
Shell 29, 34, 141, 142
situational approach *see* leadership
Slim, Field Marshal 89, 124
Sloan, Alfred 77
SMART principle 128
Snyderman, B. B. 157
Socrates 12, 29, 61, 62, 86
Sophocles 26
Stead, Bill 145
Stewart, Andrew 146
Storey, John 67
strategic leadership *see* leadership

T

Tacitus 56
Tannenbaum, R. 17, 24, 116
Tatung Co. 52
Taylor model 35
Tead, Ordway 3, 92
Telemachus 83
three-circles model
    and action-centred leadership training
        111–14, 116, 118, 120, 125–6,
        132, 149
    discussion of, 23–6
    and leadership 8, 21, 29, 33, 35, 57,
        97
    and training/development 55, 61–3,
        67, 68, 84–5, 97
Trades Union Congress 3
Truckman, Bruce 116
Twain, Mark 61

U

United Biscuits 34

V

Venn diagram 23
Vincent, Edgar 145, 146, 148, 152

W

Walker, S. 114
War
    First World 55
    Second World 17, 54
Waring, Sir Bertram 125
Wates, Neil 33
Watson, J. 8
Whiteman, M. C. 56
Woolf, Virginia 80

Z

Zaleznik, Abraham 34